A
SMALL
MOMENT
of
GREAT
ILLUMINATION

The true and lively Pourtraicture of Valentine Greatrakes Esq:, of Affane in y.ᵉ County of Waterford, in y.ᵉ Kingdome of Ireland. famous for curing several Deseases and distempers by the stroak of his Hand only.

Portrait of Valentine Greatrakes by William Faithorne
from Greatrakes' A Brief Account

A
SMALL MOMENT
of
GREAT ILLUMINATION

Searching for Valentine Greatrakes, the Master Healer

LEONARD PITT

Shoemaker *Hoard*

Library of Congress Cataloging-in-Publication Data

Pitt, Leonard.
  A small moment of great illumination : searching for Valentine Greatrakes, the master healer / Leonard Pitt.
      p. cm.
  Includes bibliographical references.
  ISBN-13: 978-1-59376-126-4
  ISBN-10: 1-59376-126-0
  1. Greatrakes, Valentine, 1629-1683. 2. Mental healing. I. Title.

RZ999.P68 2006
615.8'51-dc22

                                        2006021539

Text design by Patrick David Barber
Cover design by Gerilyn Attebery
Printed in the United States of America

Shoemaker & Hoard
An Imprint of Avalon Publishing Group, Inc.
1400 65th Street, Suite 250
AVALON Emeryville, CA 94608
Distributed by Publishers Group West

10 9 8 7 6 5 4 3 2 1

To my mother,
the memory of my father,
my brothers, and my son.
Always.

CONTENTS

A
SMALL
MOMENT
of
GREAT
ILLUMINATION

INTRODUCTION

Upon the whole, the thing is a wonderful, and stupendous,
and astonishing thing and makes us as men in a dream.
—LYONELL BEACHER, 1665

I N 1989 I CAME ACROSS A footnote in an article on the history of medicine. All it said was "Valentine Greatrakes, a seventeenth-century Irish healer." It didn't say quack or charlatan. It simply said healer. Did this man really heal? My curiosity was piqued. Some lives are changed by war or natural disaster. Others by a birth or death in the family. My life was changed by that footnote.

The next day, I ran into an acquaintance on the street, a man well versed in researching obscure corners of history. I told him of my curious find, and he suggested that maybe this man Greatrakes had written a book. I scoffed. After all, he was only a footnote. "The way to find out," he said, "is to look in the BLC." This is the British Library Catalogue, listing the millions of books in the British Library in London. "If your man was Irish and wrote anything, it's sure to be in there." "Do I have to go to London?" I asked. "No, they've got the catalog on campus." He meant Doe Library on the campus of the University of California at Berkeley, a short distance from my home. My friend noticed my hesitation and offered to take me there.

The next day, we entered the library's large reference room and walked over to the BLC, more than two hundred red-bound volumes spanning an entire wall. I pulled down the volume of Gs and thumbed quickly through the pages, and there it was, Greatrakes, Valentine. Under his name were five listings. First was *A Brief Account*, a book written by Greatrakes. Next, two books written about him, one pro and one contra. All three books were published within months of each other in early 1666. Another listing was a newspaper article about Greatrakes, dated 1665. And last, of all things, a ballad, "Rub for Rub." The latter had the note: "A reply in verse, to an attack upon the cures said to be wrought by Valentine Greatrakes." So the man had enemies. An original copy of *A Brief Account*, I learned, was in Los Angeles. But a copy of one of the books, *The Miraculous Conformist*, by Henry Stubbe, was closer at hand, at Stanford University.

My friend Iain Boal taught there. I called him that night. A few days later, we drove down to Stanford together. While Iain went off to lecture on the history of science, I walked to the rare book room and requested a copy of *The Miraculous Conformist*. This was my first visit to a library such as this. I was struck by the silence and how it differed from the silence of a regular library. Here in the rare book room, the silence was taut, full of focus and intent. In contrast to the more casual quiet of the libraries I had known, the smallest sound reverberated through the air like a violation of an ancient code.

I sat down at my assigned reading place and waited for the book to be delivered to me. It was a most slender tome, only forty pages long. A short dedication at the beginning of *The Miraculous Conformist* was signed "Stratford-upon-Avon, February 17, 1666." This book was written in Shakespeare's birthplace and barely fifty years after he died.

Valentine Greatrakes practiced an intuitive form of massage in which he would rub or stroke the body vigorously. From written affidavits signed by eyewitnesses, one learned that people felt the pain or illness move through their body until it was "run out" at the body's extremities: the hands, feet, or ears. By the time his healing talents were fully developed in 1665, Greatrakes was curing everything from blindness and deafness to leprosy and paralysis. He often failed. Many patients were cured and then relapsed. But many were cured and remained so.

On the drive back to Berkeley, I read aloud to Iain as we inched along the freeway. Stubbe's account of Greatrakes' cures challenged all credulity:

I saw him stroke a man for a pain in his left shoulder. Upon his stroking, the pain [moved] instantly into the [deltoid muscles].

THE

Miraculous Conformist:

O R

An account of severall Marvai-
lous CURES performed by the
stroaking of the Hands of

Mr VALENTINE GREATARICK;

WITH

A Physicall Discourse thereupon, In a
Letter to the Honourable *Robert Boyle* Esq;

With a Letter Relating some other of His *Miraculous Cures,*
attested by *E. Foxcroft* M.A. and Fellow of *Kings-Colledge* in *Cambr:*

B Y

HENRY STUBBE, Physician at *Strat-
ford* upon *Avon* in the County of *Warwick.*

*Non ideo negari debet quod est apertum ; quia com-
prehendi non potest quod est occultum.*

O X F O R D,

Printed by *H. Hall* Printer to the UNIVERSITY,
for *Ric: Davis,* 1 6 6 6.

Title page from Henry Stubbe's The Miraculous Conformist, *1666*

Being stroked there, it returned to the shoulder again. Upon a second stroking, it flew to the elbow, thence to his wrist, thence to his shoulder again, and thence to his fingers, whence it went out upon his last stroking so that he moved his arm vigorously every way.

Iain knew Stubbe from English history. A radical who reveled in the downfall of the monarchy in 1649, Stubbe then fled England when the throne was restored in 1660. But it was the name Robert Boyle that caused my friend to almost drive off the road.

"It looks as though Stubbe wrote this book as an open letter to Robert Boyle," I said.

"That's incredible! You must be joking!" Iain said with a start.

I obviously missed the importance of Boyle's name. Iain filled me in.

Boyle was one of the most renowned figures of his century. While he wrote prolifically on philosophy and religion, it was his work in the field of chemistry that earned him recognition as one of the founders of modern science. In 1660, he cofounded the Royal Society of London, the first institution to investigate nature according to the precepts of the new scientific method of experimentation and demonstration. His understanding of the nature of gases earned him immortality. Boyle's law, which any science major can rattle off as $PV=k$, simply means that the pressure of a gas and its volume are inversely related—as one quantity increases, the other must decrease. His research with scientist Robert Hooke into the principles of air pressure led to the invention of the air pump.

"These men have their own place in history," Iain said. "They would never associate themselves with a hoax." As much as it defied reason, these stories could not be a fabrication. The Latin proverb on the title page of Stubbe's book stood as a caution against dismissing Greatrakes outright—"Because the obscure cannot be understood, does not mean the obvious should be denied."

Iain went on about the seventeenth century, its importance in the emergence of modern science, and how this tied in to the upheavals brought about by the English Revolution, Oliver Cromwell, and so on. The image of Greatrakes and Boyle side by side stuck in my mind. Greatrakes the hands-on healer was part of an ancient tradition that would be eclipsed by the work of men just like Boyle. But who was this Greatrakes?

The thought of investigating the history of this figure was uppermost on our minds. The logic of such a pursuit made more sense for Iain than for me.

Tall with short curly hair, a wiry physique, and wire-rimmed glasses perched on his nose, Iain had the air of a man who was never far from a book. He was born in Ireland and studied at Cambridge University in England before moving to the United States. After teaching at Harvard for several years, he came to California to teach at Stanford. Forever the intrepid seeker steeped in the techniques of scholarly research, he knew what it was like to spend long hours chasing down shreds of history and to be motivated by the belief that any one of these shreds could lead to an ultimate truth, a truth that he knew the world had yet to grasp. But me? I was far from the academic type. My passion was theater and physical expression. In the 1960s, I studied mime in Paris with the master Etienne Decroux. The defining moments in my life were seeing Charlie Chaplin when I was a child, and meeting Stan Laurel at his home in Los Angeles. For years, I ran a school of physical theater in California, with students coming from around the world, and I was currently operating a theater in San Francisco.

The absurdity of launching into a project like this was only outweighed by the greater absurdity of letting it slip by. "Iain, let's do this," I said. We shook hands. For the next eight years, we tended to our lives in California while traveling back and forth between Great Britain and home to piece together the life of this enigmatic figure. This book tells Greatrakes' history as well as the strange odyssey of our search to find him.

And then there's the book—*the* book. From the very beginning of this quest, my one wish was to see an original copy of Greatrakes' book *A Brief Account.* That summer, while on tour on the East Coast, performing my one-man show, *Not for Real,* I made a side trip to Bethesda, Maryland, to the National Library of Medicine, where I knew I could see a copy of *A Brief Account.* The book was so small and unassuming. Opening the cover, I found an engraving of Greatrakes, a portrait that sparkled with clarity and brilliance. The name of the engraver surprised me: William Faithorne. One of the great artists of the period, he had also engraved the frontispiece for Thomas Hobbes' *Leviathan*.

The experience of handling an original copy of *A Brief Account*, with its handmade paper and numerous imperfections in the typesetting, and feeling its worn leather binding and the texture of the pages gave me a feel for the seventeenth century more than any historical text ever could. I imagined owning my own copy. What a thought. What chance was there of finding one? This book was published in London in 1666, only a few months before the Great Fire, and many copies were certainly lost. How many could have survived, and what were the odds that I would find one? And what about the cost? Certainly prohibitive.

As proof that we live in a world of infinite possibilities, I can now say that I do own an original copy of this book. And if the accounts of Greatrakes' cures raise any eyebrows, the extraordinary circumstances through which I found this book will undoubtedly raise the same eyebrows.

CHAPTER 1

*P*AIN AND I BEGAN reconstructing Greatrakes' life by plunging into the library system of the University of California at Berkeley. An early find was a microfilm copy of *A Brief Account*. Here was a fortunate oversight. Had I known this was in Berkeley, I might never had gone to the trouble of seeking out the original in Maryland. We also found numerous articles about Greatrakes from journals and reviews, obscure Irish and English magazines, and brief citations in scholarly works on seventeenth-century England. It didn't take long to build a picture of who this man was.

Valentine Greatrakes was born in 1628 in Affane, County Waterford, in the south of Ireland. In 1662, at age thirty-four, he discovered a talent for healing. From all evidence, he apparently did not seek this talent, nor was there any expectation that this role would ever befall him.

Healers were common in the seventeenth century and typically were poor and itinerant and received payment for their healings in some form of barter. Greatrakes, in contrast, was immensely wealthy. He never demanded payment or barter for his treatments. He was part of the Anglo-Irish gentry, with extensive landholdings on which he carried out a small industry of lumber export and beer brewing. He was also very well connected. His brother-in-law was ambassador to Spain.

The implications of his healing power were far-reaching and brought up profound issues challenging both church and state. As word of his talent spread from Ireland to England and finally to London, a great controversy rose up around him. He sat in the center of one of the great debates of his age. Many people proclaimed Greatrakes an apostle. Others denounced him as a quack. The most prominent scientists, theologians, physicians, and philosophers of the day examined him at length and struggled to find a reasoned explanation for his powers.

Along with news articles written about him in the nascent press, Greatrakes was the subject of much discussion in private correspondence. Stories of his exploits were passed on long after his death in 1683. Indeed, an entry on Greatrakes can be found in a French historical dictionary dating from 1810. Even the great P. T. Barnum spoke of him in the 1860s.

During a trip to Manhattan, I visited the New York Academy of Medicine and discovered a 1723 edition of *A Brief Account.* It too had an engraving of Greatrakes, but the portrait was a second-rate copy with none of the life of the original. The publisher's introductory comment, however, was most interesting:

> The following pamphlet being very scarce and on a very curious and uncommon subject, it is thought fit to publish it once more. It was published in 1666, a little before the great fire so that probably many copies of the impression perished in the flames. Why it was not afterwards reprinted, I am not able to give any account.

"Curious and uncommon." What an understatement.

Renowned in his own time, Greatrakes is a forgotten figure today, known only to a small circle of scholars of seventeenth-century Anglo-Irish history. Even in Ireland, he is an obscure figure. That he is known at all is largely due to his association with Robert Boyle. Volumes have been written about Boyle and his contribution to the sciences, and anyone studying Boyle in depth will come across Greatrakes.

The two men met in London in February 1666. Greatrakes had been summoned to the capital by King Charles II, who had received reports of "wondrous cures" and wanted the Irish healer examined by his royal physicians to verify that the reports were true.

Once in the capital, Greatrakes found himself in the middle of a great controversy. Of the many attacks heaped upon him, the most stinging was David Lloyd's *Wonders No Miracles*. A piece of character

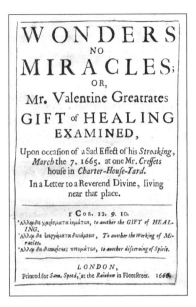

Title page from Wonders No Miracles, *an attack upon Greatrakes by David Lloyd, 1666*

assassination written anonymously, Lloyd was also well known from an earlier piece of slander, *The Countess of Bridgewater's Ghost*, a work that earned him six months in jail. Greatrakes was all the more hurt that Lloyd would level his accusations in printed form, hence a public forum.

Robert Boyle had heard of Greatrakes but, living at his manor at Stalbridge, remained above the fray. It was not until Boyle's adversary Henry Stubbe, author of *The Miraculous Conformist*, implicated the scientist in the controversy that he felt obliged to travel to London to see the healer firsthand. After careful observation, Boyle became a supporter. It was he, in fact, who encouraged Greatrakes to vindicate himself by writing a book in his own defense. Hence, the succinct *Brief Account* probably follows the advice that Boyle gave Greatrakes: Give a brief personal history, tell how you came to healing, record the names of those you treated with statements in their own words, and collect signed affidavits from witnesses who saw you cure. This approach was new to Greatrakes. He had never asked the names of those he treated, nor did he ever seek witnesses. But now, under fire, he took Boyle's advice.

But how did Greatrakes come to healing? One day in 1662, while working on his farm at Affane, he suddenly had what he called an "impulse":

> About four years since, I had an impulse or a strange persua-
> sion in my own mind, (of which I am not able to give any rational
> account to another) which did very frequently suggest to me, that
> there was bestowed on me the gift of curing the King's evil.

The king's evil is a form of tuberculosis that affects the neck and throat with large, disfiguring sores and swellings and was common in England and Ireland. The disease, also known as scrofula, was spread through contaminated milk from tubercular dairy cattle and was rampant. Often enough it was not fatal, but the disease was terribly debilitating.

Greatrakes was confused by what he called the "extraordinariness" of the impulse. For several days, he told no one and struggled to put the impulse out of his mind, but over and over, it came back to haunt him. Finally, he told his wife, Ruth, "that I did verily believe that God had given me the blessing of curing the king's evil, for whether I were in private or public, sleeping or waking, still I had the same impulse."

Ruth Greatrakes did what any commonsense woman would do if one day her husband suddenly told her he could cure a dreaded disease. She laughed. Ruth was the herbalist in the neighborhood, and her neighbors often came to her for help when they were sick. She knew what it was to care for the ill. Her husband was a landed gentleman with an enormous income of almost £1,000 a year. He had never treated anyone. She told him he had "conceived a rich fancy" and was having a "strange imagination." In terms of seventeenth-century psychology, Ruth was calling into question her husband's very sanity.

Several days later, William Maher, a neighbor from the nearby village of Salterbridge, came to the Greatrakes house with his son. Young Maher had a severe case of the evil—his throat, eye, and cheek were badly affected, and Mr. Maher was hoping that Ruth could help. Valentine took one look at the boy and stepped forward. Now his wife would see "whether this were a bare fancy or imagination as she thought" or whether it was, as he believed, "the dictates of God's spirit on my heart." He laid his hands on the boy and prayed. A few days later, Maher and his son returned. The boy's eye was "almost quite whole," and his throat was "strangely amended," wrote Greatrakes. A month later, the boy was totally healed.

News of Greatrakes' talent spread. Not long afterward, Margaret MacShane of the neighboring village of Ballinecly came to Affane. The woman suffered from a case of the king's evil that began on her stomach and spread over much of her body. "She looked so dreadfully, and stunk so exceedingly, that she would have affrighted and poisoned anyone almost that saw or came near her," Greatrakes wrote. Coincidentally, a local doctor, Doctor Anthony, was visiting the Greatrakes house that day. Valentine asked if the doctor would treat the woman, but Anthony refused, saying she was too far gone for treatment. Seeing through the doctor's motives, Greatrakes reproached him and asked him to treat MacShane for free, for God's sake, "and not to do all things for money." When Greatrakes told the doctor that he thought he could heal MacShane, the doctor replied that if he could cure the old woman, then he must be able to cure all diseases. Greatrakes disagreed, but he did think he could cure the evil. He stroked MacShane, and "my hands suppurated the nodes, and drew and healed the sores, which formerly I could not have endured the sight of, nor smell, nor touched without vomiting, so great an aversion had I naturally to all wounds and sores."

Six weeks later, a healed Margaret MacShane returned to the Greatrakes house, bearing a gift of hazelnuts to show her appreciation. For the next three years, Greatrakes tended to his lands and continued healing people stricken only with the king's evil.

Then, one day in 1664, he experienced a second impulse, this time "suggesting that there was bestowed upon me the gift of curing the ague." Ague is a malaria-like condition with symptoms of feverish sweats and chills, endemic at the time and striking down whole families. Greatrakes told his wife of this new impulse, and again she did not believe him. One can understand her skepticism at his first impulse, but with more than two years of success, one might think she would be more easily convinced. Perhaps she felt threatened that her husband's new career was usurping her position in the community as healer and caregiver.

The next day, Greatrakes was visited by a Mrs. Bateman from Fallowbridge, who suffered from the ague. He treated the woman, who "went away immediately, perfectly cured." When she returned with her husband and children, who were also sick with the disease, he treated them "in like manner, with the same success."

The third and last impulse occurred about six months later, on April 2, 1665, the Sunday morning after Easter. This time, God "was pleased to discover unto me, that he had given me the gift of healing." Greatrakes told his wife and brother about this latest impulse the next day, but still they did not believe him. From then on, he began treating all illnesses.

A few days after his last impulse, Greatrakes traveled to Lismore on business and paid a visit to his friend Cornet Dean. Having heard that Greatrakes was in the neighborhood, a neighbor of Dean's came to the door, doubled over in pain. His leg was black and covered with ulcers. The local doctors, the man said, had wanted to amputate. Greatrakes put his hand on the man's thighs "and immediately run the pains out of him so that he could stand upright without the least trouble." He laid his hand on the leg, which "changed color, and became red, and three of the five ulcers closed up, and the rest within a few hours afterwards." The man "went out well, that could hardly, by the help of his staff crawl in."

The next day, Greatrakes traveled to the village of Cahirmony in County Cork to visit to his old regimental commander, Colonel Robert Phaire. This visit proved to be a pivotal experience. Phaire was also ill with the ague and suffered from terrible hot and cold sweats. As Greatrakes treated his old friend, a group of strangers arrived at the door. One was lame, another had the falling sickness, and others had the king's evil or the ague. Greatrakes was "much amazed" that people so far away both had heard of him and knew that he could now cure many diseases. His third impulse had happened only a few days earlier, and he thought that only his brother and wife knew of this third impulse.

While he was treating Phaire's neighbors, something strange happened. For the first time, those whom Greatrakes touched felt the pain move through their body. This had never happened before. But now, he found that their pains "would skip and fly from place to place" until they exited at one of the body's extremities, the fingertips, toes, nose, eyes, mouth, or ears. All those who had come to Phaire's were healed and left rejoicing. Greatrakes was taken aback. "Lord knows, my soul was wrapt with wonder and amazement," he later wrote.

The experience at Phaire's home taught Greatrakes that the power he held in his hands was not of his own making. He believed that he was only a vessel, an instrument of God. He also knew that because this power had come to him unexpectedly, it could leave him just as abruptly. Suddenly realizing that he, from among so many others, had been given this power, he wrote that "certainly my heart melted into tears."

Not long after he began healing in 1662, Greatrakes had his first confrontation with the Catholic Church. The town of Lismore lies four miles to the west of Affane, on the Blackwater River. The bishop's court at Lismore Cathedral had heard of Greatrakes' unorthodox healings and summoned him to appear in court to be "examined." The reason had to do with money. Traditional healers and herbalists, largely women, never charged for their services, but, rather, received goods in barter. A new breed of doctors—men—were allowed to operate only with a license, which they obtained from the church, for a price. Importantly, these new doctors charged exorbitant rates for their treatments. Greatrakes' free and "irregular" cures were undercutting the profits not only of the church but of the doctors as well.

Standing before his interrogators, Greatrakes asked why he had been summoned. The church officials told him that they had received word that he had "effected cures in an extraordinary manner." They asked if this were true. Those wanting to know the truth need only come to his house for an "ocular testimony of the truth," Greatrakes replied. Better yet, he suggested, why didn't they simply ask someone he had treated? The judges asked to see Greatrakes' medical license. Greatrakes saw no reason for a license, since he never charged for his cures. Besides, he said, he knew of no law that stopped people from helping their neighbors. With no license, the judge demanded, on what authority did Greatrakes perform these acts? His only authority, he replied, was "his own strong imagination." In the end, the court told Greatrakes that practicing medicine without a license was a violation of ecclesiastical law and ordered him to stop. And so he did.

But the sick kept coming, and two days after his confrontation with the church officials, he resumed healing. Again, Greatrakes was summoned to the court at Lismore. The bishop must have realized the futility of trying to stop him altogether, because he only ordered him to stop healing within the diocese. Greatrakes protested and insisted that he would not deny help to anyone, for he "transgressed no law of God or man in doing the works of charity." There is no record of the healer's being bothered by the local clergy again.

In the summer of 1665, Greatrakes made his first foray to Dublin, the capital of the Anglo-Irish world. By now, stories of his remarkable cures had been picked up by the nascent press and were circulating throughout England and Ireland. This was the beginning of the fame and controversy that would hound him for years. A news story dated July 29, 1665, tells of Greatrakes being brought before church authorities in Dublin to be examined by a "very eminent divine." Sworn to God, Greatrakes testified that his cures were performed without the help of any charms or the devil and that he never benefited materially in any way. In the end, he was let go with no sanctions imposed against him, at least for the time being. "Indeed the clergy have not yet thought fit to prohibit him," it was stated. The word "yet" stands out as a finger-wagging threat to toe the line, or else.

Why was Greatrakes considered a threat? He threatened because the nature of his healings challenged the authority of both church and monarchy. For hundreds of years, English monarchs had performed a ritual known as the royal touch, an elaborate ceremony in which people sick with the king's evil would pass before the king to be touched on the neck, ostensibly to be healed of their disease. Each of the afflicted received a "touch piece," a gold coin strung on a ribbon to be worn around the neck as a talisman. The royal touch was part of the Crown's repertoire of propaganda created to convey the notion that the monarch's power and authority had been handed down from God—the divine right of kings.

The ceremony of the royal touch originated in the thirteenth century with Edward the Confessor and was performed continuously through the reign of Queen Anne (1701–1710), the last British monarch to carry out the ceremony. It is well known that the young Samuel Johnson was one of the last subjects to be touched. Not all English monarchs who performed the ritual were convinced of its worth. King James I was not. When he assumed the Crown in 1603, he brought with him his Calvinist skepticism. An eighteenth-century biographer wrote that James knew the ritual was only "a device to aggrandize the virtue of Kings, when miracles were in fashion; but he let the world believe it, though he smiled at it in his own reason."

Charles I

King Charles II fully understood the importance of this ritual, and within days of stepping onto English soil to restore the Crown in May 1660, he began practicing the royal touch. Over the course of his twenty-three-year reign, he touched close to one hundred thousand of his subjects. The ceremony was announced to the public by handbills posted around the city. People obtained tickets beforehand and then lined up on the appointed day and waited to be touched. So popular was the ritual that often the crowds went mad as they clamored for admission tickets. In his diary, John Evelyn recorded that, one day, "six or seven were crushed to death by pressing at the surgeon's door." Greatrakes' success at curing the king's evil put him in competition with the king.

A bit of history is needed here to explain why Greatrakes was seen as a threat to the monarchy. In August 1642, civil war broke out in England.

The execution of Charles I

King Charles I raised his battle standard at Nottingham and declared war against his enemies. One of those to oppose the king was a soldier who would distinguish himself early on: the Puritan Oliver Cromwell. After nearly six years of battle, Cromwell's forces vanquished the Royalist army. King Charles I was captured, brought to trial, and found guilty of treason and murderous acts against the people of England. On January 30, 1649, he was led to the scaffold and beheaded at Whitehall before a stunned crowd of thousands. The monarchy was abolished, and for the next eleven years, England was governed by Oliver Cromwell's protectorate. When Cromwell died in 1658, power was supposed to pass into the hands of his son Richard, but he proved too feeble to govern. Events devolved from there, and in May 1660, the monarchy was restored. Charles II entered London to the acclaim of the population, and as mentioned previously, one of his first acts to bolster his legitimacy was to reinstate the ceremony of the royal touch.

Six years later, Greatrakes was performing the same act and with a high rate of success. Was he part of a radical sect trying to embarrass the king and demystify his power? Was he working to overthrow the monarchy? In the mid-1660s, there were still strong fears that subversive groups might rise up again to topple the monarchy. To complicate matters, Greatrakes had served in Cromwell's army in Ireland, a fact not lost on the Royalists of the Restoration. This association was to harass him continually.

One day, Iain and I took stock. Greatrakes' cures, well documented as they seemed, were still an enigma. Had there been only a few reports of cures, they could be explained away. But there were so many, from different times and places, corroborated and signed by the most respected men of the period. What conclusion could we draw? A prominent San Francisco psychiatrist, a student of medical history familiar with Greatrakes, dismissed him as a paranoid schizophrenic. A truly remarkable diagnosis. Were this true, what does it say about Boyle? Was he a mere dupe? What about others who signed on as eyewitnesses—people such as the poet Andrew Marvell and the neo-Platonist philosopher

Henry More, Isaac Newton's teacher and the first to translate Descartes into English? Even Thomas Sydenham, the father of modern clinical medicine and the most respected physician of the era, vouched for Greatrakes. And the list goes on. One could not summon a more illustrious list of personalities to stand in one's defense.

When confronting strange phenomena such as those surrounding Greatrakes, it is often the skeptics who offer the most interesting testimony. Contrary to what we might think today, Greatrakes' contemporaries, living in an age before science, were not an entirely gullible lot ready to believe any superstition or claim of the supernatural. Many were skeptical and demanded proof. One such skeptic was Lyonell Beacher of Youghal, a port town at the mouth of the Blackwater River on the Irish Sea. In 1665, a report by Beacher, *Wonders If Not Miracles*, was published in London. Not willing to believe the reports of Greatrakes' cures, he traveled to Affane to see for himself. Greatrakes treated people three days a week, from six in the morning until six in the evening. He laid his hands "on all that came so that my stable, barn, and malthouse, were filled with sick people and many were cured and many were not."

Beacher described how he was convinced by seeing Greatrakes' actions in person:

> Sir, Having heard of many diseases healed and cured by
> Valentine Gertrux of Affane, [many] of them seemed so strange to
> me, that I could not give credit to the reports till I went up [there]
> myself. . . . [I] stood close by him, and saw him touch many of the

King's Evil and many also whom he had cured of that distemper came to acknowledge it, which is the utmost reward he accepts from any. I saw him heal eight persons of the dead palsy in their arms and legs, whom after he had touched and stroked them, he caused to be lifted up, and they had instantly the right use of their limbs. I also saw him restore many deaf persons to their hearing and this only by stroking and putting his fingers into the holes of their ears. [And] had I not been, I think I should not have believed, though all the people in Youghal had told me of it.

As word of Greatrakes' powers reached England, boatloads of diseased people sailed to Ireland to seek his touch. Travelers arrived at the port at Youghal, took a small vessel up the Blackwater River, disembarked at Cappoquin, and then doubled back the mile to Affane, either on foot or on litters. The number of people clamoring at Greatrakes' door in Affane was so great that the neighboring towns could not accommodate them. To make himself more accessible to the crowds, he left Affane and moved down to Youghal, "where great multitudes resorted to me, not only of the inhabitants, but also out of England."

In the summer of 1665, a Dublin newspaper, *The Intelligencer*, carried a report by another skeptic who had gone to Youghal to observe Greatrakes:

My curiosity would not permit me to refrain from beholding Mr. Valentine Greatrakes, curing of all diseases in this town. In short, the multitudes that follow, and the press of people are only for those to believe that see it. Two or three ships well freighted out of England with all diseases, are most returned well home. He is forced to leave his own house, and lives at Youghal, through necessity that throng after him.

Youghal was a relatively large city, a commercial center with more lodgings to house the crowds. The plague was rampant in London that summer, with hundreds dying daily, and while Greatrakes does not mention the plague explicitly, from all reports it appears he did treat the disease. Fearful that some of the sick "might bring the infection" with them, he wrote, the Youghal magistrates forced him to return to Affane. Back home, he continued treating the ill and wrote that he could not "remember that in all that time any one of my family was ever infected by them. Neither did any of them, though they herded together, infect one the other."

Reading Greatrakes' history gave rise to a string of questions. What was he actually doing? Was he a master hypnotist? Were people being cured by their own imagination? Was he tricking people into being cured? Maybe the cures were simply a coincidence—the people would have gotten better, anyway. Was he so charismatic that he could induce a state of euphoria or self-healing in his patients? The claims that he was a charlatan are countered by the fact that he never charged for his treatments. What's more, he put himself to great trouble to treat people.

How much does belief have to do with it? Was Greatrakes able to heal because people believed that he could heal? People believed many things in the seventeenth century—things that seem strange today. Robert Boyle, like others on the vanguard of the new science, still believed in the old folk traditions, such as the belief that some illnesses could be cured by placing a dead man's hand on the chest of a sick person. What about the skeptics who submitted to Greatrakes' stroking reluctantly and whose condition improved dramatically? Everywhere we turned, we met a challenge. Maybe, as some believe, it was just psychological.

Through the course of our research, Iain and I compiled a long list of items we wanted to see: original manuscripts and books that could only be found in the archives in Ireland and England. A letter written by a contemporary of Greatrakes' purporting to expose his "imposture" sat in the British Library. Then, too, there was the ballad "Rub for Rub," defending Greatrakes against the attack of a London doctor. What other pieces of evidence might we discover?

And there was the land. The place names of the Greatrakes story— Affane, Cappoquin, Wormhill, Lismore—stood out like lures to my imagination. We found Affane on a modern map of Ireland, but what would the place be like today, three hundred years after Greatrakes lived there? Is there anything left standing from Greatrakes' time? And there was *A Brief Account*. My desire to own a copy of this book had grown. My fantasy as I rambled through old bookstores was to find a copy on a musty bookshelf for five or ten dollars. News stories of great literary finds in the most unusual places fueled my search. A handwritten draft of Mark Twain's *Huckleberry Finn* was found in an old trunk stored away in a Hollywood apartment. An original copy of the Declaration of Independence was found on the back of a picture frame at a garage sale. Short of a similar miracle, wouldn't I have a better chance of finding the book in Great Britain?

I ran into my friend again, the acquaintance who got me started on this odyssey in the first place. I told him of our progress, what we had uncovered, and what we had yet to find. Fittingly, the last thing he said as we parted was "Get thee to Ireland!"

Iain and I then decided the only reasonable thing to do was to make the journey, and as soon as possible. Doing this out of our own pocket with no grant or institutional support of any kind was lunacy—we knew that—but we had no choice. Rearrange schedules, scrape the money together, do whatever it took, but make the journey. We needed at least a month to comb through the archives and visit all the places on our list. The harsh reality of our schedules only allowed us a short nine days.

CHAPTER 2

*A*S IAIN AND I STUDIED the many accounts of Greatrakes' healings, we became very good at shaking our heads and rolling our eyes. We had long ceased trying to find explanations for things that were clearly inexplicable. All we could do was proceed with Stubbe's admonition in mind: "Because the obscure cannot be understood, does not mean the obvious should be denied." Nevertheless, we proceeded with a very unsettled feeling. Sure, the facts of this history were solid—the people were real, reputable to a fault—but there was an air of unreality to it all. Had we been living in California too long? Iain reassured me. "It doesn't make any difference whether it was real or not. It's not for us to decide. That's not the point. Greatrakes is part of a history that deserves and needs to be told. Not only for his own story but for the larger history that he illuminates. All we have to do is keep working. People will draw their own conclusions."

In the weeks before our departure, Iain and I worked feverishly to gain as much information about Greatrakes as possible. His first name comes from the simple fact that he was born on Valentine's Day. But Greatrakes? The name derives from the hamlet where the family originated in the region of Derbyshire in central England. The major industry in this region was mining, and *rake* is a mining term signifying a cleft or fissure in the rock from which lead ore was mined. The community, Great Rakes, was a grouping of only three or four farmhouses near the village of Wormhill, a name we added to our list of places to visit.

As the story of the Greatrakes family unfolded, it became clear that this history illuminated a much larger history, that of England and Ireland and the bloody hyphen that joins Anglo to Irish. For example, in the 1580s, Greatrakes' paternal grandfather, William, traveled to Ireland as a soldier in Queen Elizabeth's army—part of a massive military operation to colonize the south of Ireland. In this scheme, known as the Munster Plantation, the British used Ireland as a laboratory to test techniques of colonization—techniques they would later adapt to other countries around the world to build their global empire. William Greatrakes was made deputy commissary of victuals, the person responsible for supplying foodstuffs to the troops.

This invasion of Ireland was not simply a war of English against Irish, or Protestant against Catholic. The Catholic population in Ireland consisted of both Gaelic Irish and Old English. Many of these Old English, descendants of the Anglo-Normans who invaded Ireland in the twelfth century and stayed, were some of the largest landowners in Ireland. This group was in the ambiguous position of being Irish by culture and religion, yet English by ancestry. Depending on their religious allegiance, these Old English families were seen by the Protestant English Crown as sometimes friend, sometimes foe.

William Greatrakes received payment for his services to the Crown with a grant of land confiscated from the Irish in County Waterford on the west bank of the Blackwater River, at what was then known as New Affane. There, he married Ann Croker and constructed a fortified house known as Norrisland Castle to defend his family from the hostile Irish neighbors. Iain and I found this house on a nineteenth-century map of the area. Was it still standing? We added it to our list of places to visit.

William Greatrakes was an industrious farmer with large fruit orchards. He was the first person in Ireland to produce apple cider, for which he was renowned throughout the country. He exported his cider abroad to India, the West Indies, and other foreign lands.

Valentine's father, also named William, was born in 1573 and, like the senior William, entered into the service of the English Crown, where he received high administrative appointments in the province of Munster as clerk of the Crown and clerk of the peace. Aside from his civic duties at home, he was a gentleman farmer who managed his substantial estate, looked after his Irish tenants, and collected rents.

He married Mary Harris, also Anglo-Irish. Her father, Sir Edward Harris, was second justice of the King's Bench in Ireland and subsequently chief justice of Munster, the highest office in the English judicial system in Ireland. Together, they had five children. Valentine was the oldest. William died when Valentine was four years old.

In October 1641, when Valentine was only thirteen years old, the native Irish rose up in a massive and bloody rebellion to expel their English colonizers. Whole towns and villages were overrun, houses were burned, and many Protestants were killed. This struggle for liberation dragged on for almost fifteen years. The English treatment of the Irish illustrates the Irish case for freedom. In County Waterford, English soldiers led a hundred Irish prisoners to Cappoquin village, one mile north of Affane. The soldiers tied their captives in twos, back to back; cast them into the river; and "made sport to see them drowned." In County Cork, Dennis Downey was gelded, had one eye pulled out, and was then "sent in that posture to his wife." In April, a blind woman of eighty years was placed on a bed of straw, "to which they set fire and so burnt her. The same day they hanged two women in Kilbride, and two old decrepit men that begged alms of them." The Irish reciprocated with like brutality.

The catalyst for this rebellion was the fragile state of the monarchy in England. As the English state foundered in mid-1641, the Crown's authority in Ireland grew weak, which in turn provided the opportunity

THE TRIUMPHANT RETURN OF THE ENGLISH SOLDIERS
From *The Image of Irelande* by John Derricke

English soldiers returning triumphantly from war in Ireland

for the Irish to rise up. At the outbreak of the rebellion, Greatrakes' mother, Mary, fled to England with her children and sought refuge with her brother Edmund Harris. The young Greatrakes had just finished his primary education at the Free School in Lismore and was planning to attend Trinity College in Dublin, but with the country in chaos, these plans evaporated.

In England, Valentine undertook his religious education with his uncle Edmund, a devout Protestant. When his uncle died in 1646, five years after the onset of the Irish rebellion, Valentine continued his education in the village of Stoke Gabriel on the River Dart, where he studied Humanity and Divinity with a High-German minister, John Daniel Getseus.

Iain and I added Stoke Gabriel to our list of places to visit.

The respite Mary Greatrakes found in England did not last long, for barely a year later, England fell into its own civil war. Sometime around 1646–1647, as both England and Ireland continued hemorrhaging with their separate wars, Greatrakes, then nearly twenty years old, decided to leave his mother and siblings in England. He return to Ireland to try to regain the family land that had been lost to the Irish rebels during the rebellion. "I determined to return to Ireland, and there either regain my estate, or lose my life."

Greatrakes had heard stories of the civil war in Ireland, yet was totally unprepared for the devastation he found. Years of brutal conflict had left the country in ruins, and the war was far from over. The rebellion had produced, he wrote, "strange divisions [of] English against English, and Irish against Irish, and Protestants and Papists joining hands in one province, against the Protestants of another." Greatrakes was so traumatized by the carnage that he fell into a state of deep depression and secluded himself for a year in the castle of Cappoquin, where he lived "in contemplation . . . till the mist of confusion was over":

> I saw so much of the madness and wickedness of the world,
> that my life became a burden to me . . . my soul was as weary of
> this habitation of clay as ever the galley-slave was of the oar, which
> brought my life to the threshold of death, so that my legs had
> hardly strength to carry my enfeebled body about.

During this period of Greatrakes' isolation in 1648, the English civil war came to an end. The Irish could draw no comfort from the English Revolution that dethroned the monarchy, for the policy of the new English government toward Ireland remained as violent as before. Cromwell (Protestant), along with the Puritans, looked upon the Irish (Catholic) as infidels deserving of the same holy war that the Crusades had brought to the Holy Land. Cromwell also hated the Irish because he believed they had killed many Protestants during the 1641 rebellion. Within less than a year of coming to power, Cromwell prepared a full-scale invasion of Ireland. In August 1649, he landed in Youghal with a massive force ready to deal with the Irish problem. He set about massacring not only the native Irish, but also English Royalists who had fled to Ireland after the overthrow of the monarchy.

Greatrakes emerged from his self-imposed seclusion at this time, and in a surprising move, enlisted as a cavalry officer in Cromwell's army. He was commissioned a lieutenant in the regiment of Colonel Robert Phaire under the command of Robert Boyle's brother, Roger, the Earl of Orrery. What a strange twist. The young man who a year earlier had been appalled to the point of death by the violence had now joined in the butchery.

During the years-long war, many people took advantage of the turmoil to take possession of land that was not their own. A portion of the Greatrakes estate at Affane had been wrongfully claimed by a Captain Hennessey, who fraudulently collected rents there. In a letter dated 1649,

Greatrakes petitioned the Duke of Ormonde for return of his family lands on the Blackwater, "which my predecessors formerly have enjoyed and was before [these] unhappy distractions in my father's possession."

While Greatrakes and his regiment remained in the south of Ireland, Cromwell headed north with a large force to attack the rebel stronghold at Drogheda. There he laid siege to the town and, after two concentrated assaults, penetrated the rebel defenses. His vengeance upon the Irish inhabitants was merciless. Over a period of two days, his army butchered more than three thousand men, women, and children. Thirty-five people survived the bloodbath and were shipped off to Barbados as slaves. In a letter to England after the battle, Cromwell acquitted himself of this black deed by writing that he was "persuaded that this [victory] is a righteous judgment of God upon these barbarous wretches," and that it would "prevent the effusion of blood for the future," a justification for war used many times since. Greatrakes, in contrast, claimed that during his military service, he was careful to never "oppress or injure any [prisoners] that were in [my protection] . . . nor did I permit any women or children to be killed . . . where I had a power to restrain the fury of the soldier."

Burrowing through a multitude of obscure journals, I came across a report of a military action that Greatrakes had conducted in November 1654. During Cromwell's rule, any Catholic priest found conducting the Mass in Ireland was considered an outlaw. These priests were routinely hunted down, arrested, and shipped off to Barbados. Their captors received the substantial sum of £5 per head. Greatrakes and his soldiers had discovered a priest hiding in a castle in County Meath. They tried to arrest the man but were driven back by his defenders. After a short skirmish, Greatrakes and his men succeeded in entering the castle and took the priest into custody. Greatrakes seized all the property belonging to those who defended the clergyman and distributed it among his soldiers as plunder. The fate of the priest is unknown.

By 1653 Cromwell had succeeded in crushing the Irish rebellion and began dividing up the lands he had confiscated from the rebels. Again he demonstrated how little difference there was between the monarchy he had toppled and the Puritan regime over which he reigned. Cromwell had a long list of wealthy English "adventurers" (investors) waiting to stake their claim to Irish lands. Standing in their way, however, were the thousands of English soldiers who expected these lands as payment for their military service. The Cromwellian government, favoring the adventurers, concocted a scheme to eliminate the soldiers. The English state invited foreign envoys from Spain, France, and Poland to Ireland to hire English mercenaries to fight in their own wars. The carrot of immediate employment worked, and over forty thousand English soldiers enlisted abroad. With this obstacle out of the way, the government stepped in and began expropriating large portions of Irish land that it later gave away to its favorites. These lands were not vacant. They had been inhabited for centuries by the native Irish, who rightfully claimed them as their own.

Like their ancestors before them, the native Irish were driven off their land and exiled into Connaught, west of the Shannon River. In the early autumn of 1653, the sound of beating drums signaled the beginning of the Irish deportation, which continued through the winter until springtime. Harsh restrictions were established in Connaught to control the Irish with heavy penalties for any infraction. Everyone had to obey a rigorous passport system. No Irish were allowed to be seen within two miles of the Shannon, or four miles of the Atlantic Ocean. Anyone found dodging the system was put to death without trial. A rigid program of identification was also established. Irish noblemen were forced to wear an identifying mark on their clothing, and persons of lesser rank were marked with a black spot on the right cheek. Enforcement of these restrictions was difficult, but their enactment starkly portrays the historically oppressive policy of the English toward the Irish. The English also made a business of slavery by selling off thousands of young Irish girls to planters in the West Indies.

In 1656, Greatrakes' regiment was disbanded and his seven-year stint in the military came to an end: "I then betook myself to a country life, and lived at Affane, the habitation of my ancestors, where I have continued ever since, and got by my industry a livelihood out of the bowels of the earth."

With the war over, Greatrakes' former regimental commander, Robert Phaire, was made governor of County Cork. As a sign of friendship, Phaire appointed Greatrakes to the civic posts of clerk of the peace, justice of the peace, and register for transplantation. As register for transplantation, Greatrakes had the gruesome task of seeing to it that the Irish vacated their lands so the property could be occupied by the arriving English settlers. In cases where the Irish refused their deportation orders, force was used.

My first encounter with Phaire was in *A Brief Account*. At first glance, he did not appear important. But a little digging revealed otherwise. To my surprise, Phaire was a regicide (the term comes from *regi*, "king," and *cide*, "murder"). He was among those who had signed the death warrant for King Charles I in 1649. Phaire's role in the king's execution places him at the center of one of the most dramatic events in English history. His survival into the Restoration suggests that he was an extremely lucky man. Not all of his cohorts did so well.

A short recap will help show just how lucky he was. Upon restoring the monarchy, King Charles II began hunting down the regicides who had murdered his father. Some had died, some had emigrated to America, and others had fled to the continent. Those who were captured were convicted of high treason and faced a monstrous fate. In its civility, the English court chose not to hang the regicides. Rather, it only half hanged them. One by one, the condemned men mounted the scaffold. A rope was placed around their neck and drawn up slowly so as to strangle them into a delirious, yet conscious state. Then they were let down, to have their genitals and entrails cut out and held up before their eyes and burned. This done, the man was beheaded and quartered. The body parts were displayed on the city gates for all to see.

Phaire was hunted down and captured in Dublin on May 18, 1660, a mere sixteen days after the Restoration. In June, he was sent to the Tower of London, where he was tried and, remarkably, exonerated for his part in the king's execution. What could account for such an extraordinary turn of events? It can only be surmised that Phaire was saved because of . . . his wife. In 1658, about a month before Cromwell died, Phaire married Elizabeth Herbert. Anyone intimate with the history of King Charles I's trial and execution would recognize the name immediately. I did not. Elizabeth Herbert was the daughter of Sir Thomas Herbert, who was attendant to Charles I during the last hours of the king's life. It is nothing less than a mystery how Phaire, a virulent anti-Royalist, came to marry a woman from the very heart of the English royalty. A possible explanation is that Phaire knew that the monarchy would probably be restored after Cromwell's death and that he, a regicide, would be in dire trouble. What better way of improving his chances for survival than by marrying into a Royalist family? But then, how did he even gain entry into a circle so deeply Royalist?

Only days before our departure, Iain phoned me. "Leonard, I've got something that might interest you," he said, with characteristic understatement. "Can I pop over?" Iain walked in and handed me a book, *The Conway Letters*. Never heard of it. He opened the book to a full page of the Faithorne engraving of Greatrakes. I was stunned. Not only that, but the entire chapter was entitled "Valentine Greatrakes." The book comprises the correspondence of Lord Edward and Viscountess Anne Conway, a seventeenth-century aristocratic couple who lived at Ragley Hall, in the region of Warwickshire, in central England.

A friend of Iain's had heard of our work on the seventeenth century and suggested that we consult the book. We might find something interesting, he said. Indeed. This friend didn't even know we were working on Greatrakes, and here was an entire chapter about the healer. This wonderful book, published in 1930, was written by Marjorie Hope Nicolson, a young American scholar from Yonkers. Nicolson spent eighteen summers in London at the British Library during the 1910s and 1920s, poring over the family correspondence of Edward and Anne Conway.

The Conways were part of the English elite and had a circle of friends made up of some of the most prominent figures of the period. Periodically, the group would meet at Ragley to discuss the most burning questions of the day in the fields of religion, science, and medicine. The person to preside over this highly esteemed gathering was not Edward Conway, but rather Anne Conway.

Lady Conway was one of the most interesting figures of her time. While her gender would not allow her a university education, she attained, through her own dogged perseverance, a level of intellectual development to rival any man of her day. She taught herself Greek and Latin and mastered the classics of both languages.

Anne Conway also suffered from terrible migraine headaches. At age twelve, she contracted a serious illness from which she recovered, but the episode left her with debilitating headaches that worsened with time. By the mid-1660s, she was in her thirties, and her migraines had become so severe that she was often confined to bed for weeks at a time. Edward Conway had heard of Greatrakes and arranged for him to come to Ragley in January 1666 so as to attempt a cure. Stubbe, a friend of the Conways', was one of a group of men invited to Ragley to witness Greatrakes, and it was there that Stubbe and Greatrakes met.

Over the years, Anne Conway sought relief for her migraines from every respectable physician in England, including her kin William Harvey, discoverer of the circulation of the blood. He suggested that she try the dreaded treatment of trepanning: boring a hole in the skull to drain off a small amount of fluid to relieve pressure, and this in an age before anesthetics. She resigned herself to the ordeal and made arrangements to travel to Paris to see the trepanning "specialists." At the last minute, however, she balked and the operation was never performed, although the French physicians did open her jugular artery. On a later occasion, at the suggestion of the chemist Robert Hues, she submitted to the mercury treatment, swallowing a vial of mercury, with near-fatal results. Robert Boyle, too, was a friend of the family and attempted a cure by preparing his well-known concoction, *Ens veneris*, which also produced no results. Other attempted cures included the continuous dripping of water on the head, the ingestion of the liquid form of opium— laudanum—and even the two newest of drugs, tobacco and coffee.

Some years earlier, Edward Conway had attempted another cure on his wife, one performed not by a person, but rather by a stone. In 1658, during an almost fatal bout of her "sad affliction," Anne fantasized that she was pregnant. Edward was prone to such fantasies of his own—"We have had thoughts oftentimes in my wife's sickness, perhaps she may be breeding." Even though the best doctors and midwives

A painting of Viscountess Conway by Samuel Van Hoogstraaten

assured them this was not so, and Edward himself had long since given up on any "impetuous desires after children," he asked his brother-in-law Sir George Rawdon to send from Ireland, by express messenger and in secret ("that we may not be made a town-talk") "an eagle's stone esteemed of great virtue in hard labour." This stone was believed to have "that eminent property to promote delivery or restrain abortion, respectively applied to lower or upward parts of the body."

During the summer of 1665, Edward Conway began receiving correspondence from colleagues in Ireland about sensational cures they had seen Greatrakes perform. Conway immediately contacted his circle in Dublin to verify the stories. Satisfied that Greatrakes was authentic, he asked Rawdon to make arrangements for the healer to come to Bristol, "where my horses shall meet him and bring him hither." But Greatrakes had no desire to travel abroad and declined the offer. Conway then wrote to his friend the archbishop of Dublin, Robert Boyle's cousin, and asked him to intercede as well. This was a poor choice. The archbishop had only contempt for Greatrakes. He agreed to the meeting out of friendship for Conway and "not out of any expectation that he could in any way be conducible to your Ladyes health."

In their meeting, the archbishop condescendingly allowed Greatrakes the "supposition that many of his pretended cures were really performed" and questioned him about the origin of his strange power, whether it was God or the devil. Greatrakes denied that his power had anything to do with the devil. The conversation between the two men ended abruptly with Greatrakes telling the archbishop that he, Greatrakes, "would not go thither for any Lord whomsoever." The archbishop wrote to Conway, telling him of "all the impertinencys that passed between us" and that he looked upon Greatrakes as a man laboring "under a strong delusion, and infinitely misguided by his own imagination."

But Edward Conway would not be deterred. A friend of his in Dublin, the Earl of Orrery, was Greatrakes' former army commander. Perhaps an appeal from him would help. Greatrakes admired the earl, but remained steadfast in refusing to make the trip. With winter approaching, he knew the journey would be long, difficult, and possibly dangerous. Besides, he did not want to leave his wife and family for so long a time. Orrery resorted to offering a substantial reward, but still Greatrakes refused. The healer had never accepted payment for his treatments and would not begin now. Orrery insisted that the payment was not for treating Anne Conway, but was only a reimbursement for the expense of being away from his family. Greatrakes finally relented but was apprehensive that people would think poorly of his receiving payment:

> I know it will seem strange to all who know me, that I who
> never received pension or gratuity from any man hitherto, should
> propose anything of a reward to myself now. But I hope when it's
> rightly considered, how that I run the hazards of the enraged seas,
> the winter . . . and forego the comfort of my family, it will not
> seem strange.

Greatrakes sailed for England in early January 1666.

Keys to our research were the many footnotes that we stumbled upon and that led to important sources we might otherwise have missed. One such footnote referred to an 1880 edition of the British magazine *Argosy* with an article about Greatrakes' stay at Ragley. Without going to England, I despaired of finding a copy. At Iain's suggestion, I searched Doe Library. And there it was.

The magazine contained an account of Greatrakes' visit to Ragley—an account written with startling detail more than two hundred years after the fact by a C. J. Langston, a man who claims to know "somewhat more than most people" about the history of Ragley. How he could know so much about what happened there so long ago is a mystery, more so since he provides no clues about how he acquired the information. With this proviso, the fascinating account is nevertheless worth a look.

Greatrakes found the winter sea crossing to England every bit as bad as, and in fact worse than, he expected. The ship was driven so far off course that everyone feared the old vessel would go down. When the ship finally landed on the coast of Somersetshire, Greatrakes was surrounded by people who recognized him and were "anxious to witness some token of his powers."

Greatrakes arrived at Ragley on January 27, 1666. "It was a dull day threatening snow, and a sharp north wind had fringed the river Arrow with ice." As he rode up to the estate, a small group of tenants on the land stood at the entrance, waiting to catch a glimpse of the renowned healer. He was received by Edward Conway, Doctor Taylor, and Francis Mercury Van Helmont, son of the famous chemist. The small group accompanied him up the long path to the mansion, walking alongside his horse. A number of the Conway's distinguished friends assembled at Ragley to witness the healer: Conway's brother-in-law George Rust, Henry More, Ralph Cudworth, Benjamin Whitchcote, John Worthington, and Henry Stubbe.

In his article, Langston attributes Anne Conway's inclination toward the mystical to her infirm condition, in which "there was too much mind for the body" and thus her "fragile form was laid aside for weeks together." He then makes an enigmatic allusion to the use of drugs or some other kind of mind-altering agent: "Thus she sometimes lived 'out of body,' by becoming habituated to certain influences which produced startling effects."

Before trying his powers on Anne Conway, Greatrakes spent several days treating the Conways' tenants, who were eager to see him. In the Conway family correspondence, Edward vouches for the success of these cures. Greatrakes then approached Lady Anne.

> They sat together one morning in her chamber talking at length. Greatrakes was glad to see the sun shining, "for," he said, "the sun, madam, is a great healer and composer." Passing his right hand somewhat quickly down the spine, he inquired whether the patient felt a sensation of smarting. She said, "No!" Presently he pressed one hand on the temples, and stroked the back of the head with the other; afterwards gently clasping the wrists.

For a moment, Lady Conway's pain subsided, only to return again with greater force.

Greatrakes spent about two weeks at Ragley. His repeated attempts to alleviate Anne's pain met with failure. Edward wrote of his disappointment to his brother-in-law George Rawdon, but also of successful cures he had seen Greatrakes perform:

> Mr. Gratrax hath been here a fortnight tomorrow, and my wife is not the better for him. Very few others have failed under his hands, of many hundreds he hath touched in these parts. I must confess that before his arrival, I did not believe the tenth part of those things which I have been an eye-witness of, and several others who are come hither out of curiosity, do acknowledge his operations.

The one friend in Anne Conway's circle certain to be most disappointed with Greatrakes' failure was philosopher Henry More, Isaac Newton's teacher and the first person to translate Descartes into English. Conway's intense desire for learning led her into a friendship with More, who became her mentor and closest confidant. The two carried on a lengthy correspondence centered on the question of Descartes' new system of thought, just then coming into vogue. Over the years, when he wasn't teaching at Cambridge, More would pay her long visits at Ragley Hall.

As Conway matured, she developed a strong mystical inclination and a belief in spiritualism. She even believed that one could commune with disembodied spirits and that they could communicate among themselves as well. Lady Conway's mysticism led her to ultimately reject a belief in the separation of spirit and flesh, and it was on this question of separation that she differed with Descartes. Separation of mind and body was anathema to her way of thinking, and after an initial period of fascination, she rejected the French philosopher's thought entirely. Toward the end of her life, Conway left the Church of England to become a Quaker, a conversion that greatly sorrowed her friend More.

After her death in 1678, a compilation of her writings on the history of philosophy was published, but because of the subordinate position of women, her name was not allowed on the title page. Instead, her friend and physician, Van Helmont, was recognized as the book's author. It was only many years later that the true mind behind these writings was revealed.

To Edward Conway's credit, he still vouched for Greatrakes' healing power despite the failure to cure his wife. In another letter to Rawdon, Conway described an astonishing cure he had witnessed when Greatrakes healed a young boy stricken with leprosy. The boy was covered from head to foot with the disease,

> which had been judged incurable above ten years, and in my
> chamber he cured him perfectly, that is, from a moist humor, t'was
> immediately dried up, and began to fall off, the itching was quite
> gone, and the heat of it taken away. The youth was transported to
> admiration.

In a rare instance of two independent reports of the same cure, Henry Stubbe also witnessed this cure and wrote his own account, which he included in *The Miraculous Conformist.* Several days after the first treatment, the boy returned to Ragley to see Greatrakes, and Stubbe recorded these observations:

> The moist salt and brinish humor which caused a moist leprosy was dried up, and in some places scaled off. The skin under it was red. There was no itching or pricking at all, nor heat, with which symptoms he had been formerly troubled. Mr. Greatarick stroked him again, and rubbed his body all over with spittle. My Lord ordered the boy to return, if he were not cured, but he came back no more.

As the debate around Greatrakes raged on, people struggled to find an explanation for his power. Some speculated that it had to do with his physical makeup and constitution. People remarked on his robustness and healthy mien. One writer noted that he had "a majestical, yet affable presence, a lusty body, and a composed carriage." Another described him as "a strong man, of a sanguine temperament and very healthy." Sixty years after Greatrakes' death, Robert Phaire's son recollected that "Mr. Greatrakes was of a large stature, and surprising strength. He has very often taken a handful of hazel-nuts and crack'd most of them with one grip of his hand, and has often divided a single hazel-nut by his thumb and fore-finger. He had the largest, heaviest, and softest hand, I believe, of any man of his time."

Stubbe was certain that Greatrakes' healing powers were in part due to the particular makeup of his body. As proof, he cited reports of Greatrakes' body exuding a sweet, aromatic scent. One morning, Edward Conway entered Greatrakes' room and observed "a smell strangely pleasant, as if it had been of sundry flowers." He asked the servant what "sweet water" he had brought into the room and was told, none. Even Greatrakes' urine was examined and was found to smell like violets, "though he had eaten nothing that might give it that scent."

Stubbe also speculated that if illness can be transmitted by touch, is it not possible to transmit an excess of health? Perhaps Greatrakes was transmitting his own health to the people he treated. The term used to describe this phenomenon was *sanative contagion.* The agent thought to be transmitted was an *effluvia* created from the friction of his rubbing, which in turn stimulated the patient's physical constitution like a tonic or an elixir.

Henry Oldenburg, secretary of the Royal Society, subscribed to this belief, as he explained in a letter to Robert Boyle: "Greaterix does certainly some cures by friction, insinuating (perhaps) some salubrious stream or spirits of his own into sickly people's bodies."

Others suspected that he had some type of medicine or salve that he concealed in his hands and then applied to the body. Stubbe observed Greatrakes carefully and wrote "there was no manner of fraud, and his hands had no manner of medicaments upon them, for I smelled them and handled them, and saw them washed more than once after some cures, and before others."

More important, though, were the theological implications of Greatrakes' power. Many struggled to find a reasoned explanation for the cures within an ecclesiastical framework. Were the cures miracles? If so, this threatened the hierarchy of the church, for miracles were only possible through God's official representatives and not through spontaneous manifestations among laypeople. If Greatrakes' cures were not miracles, but rather were due to the healing power of nature, then what did this say about the miracles of the saints, the apostles, and even Jesus himself? Perhaps these wonders, too, had a natural explanation. Was Greatrakes a religious radical trying to reduce these figures to the level of common faith healers? If his cures were miracles, did this mean that Greatrakes must be elevated to the level of an apostle? Every line of questioning led to a dead end.

If Greatrakes' healings were not the work of God, were they the work of the devil? If the cures were miraculous, why were some people cured with great ease and others with great effort? But, then again, wasn't the age of miracles supposedly over? If the cures were not miracles, then they must have had a natural cause. This was untenable. To the seventeenth-century mind, nature had no inherent power to heal. Only God could heal. And on and on went the questioning.

Greatrakes does not say as much about the subject as we would like. *A Brief Account* is written in a style so terse, almost like a piece of impressionism, that we are left with more questions than answers. While Greatrakes never spoke of his cures as miracles, he did believe that his power to cure was a combination of the divine and the natural. His ability to heal, he wrote, was a gift bestowed upon him by God. Greatrakes was certain of this because "I am very sensible of the particular time when this gift was bestowed on me, before which time I had it not." But the cures themselves, he thought, were effected by natural means—effluvias emanating from a particular "temper of body" that God had given him: "I suppose that no man will question but that an extraordinary gift may be exercised by natural means, or that God may confer in an extraordinary manner such a temper of body upon a person, as may, by a natural efficacy, produce these effects."

Whatever explanation Greatrakes offered for his power, it was never enough for his contemporaries. Why, he was asked, would God choose him to perform cures in such an extraordinary manner? If the cures were God's work, why were some people cured at once, and others not at all? Why would the pains "fly immediately out of some, and take such ambages in others?" Why would the illness leave some people at their eyes, some at their fingers, some at their toes, some at their noses, and others at their ears or mouths?

To those who sat in judgment upon him, Greatrakes hoped that *A Brief Account* would "prove a bridle to their tongues." These people, he said, thought they belonged to "God Almighty's privy council," yet they had less "religion" than they did "confidence." Otherwise, they would have been "less presumptuous" than to question God's will. As to why some people were cured at a single touch and others were not, he replied, "If all these things could have a plain and rational account then [there] would be no reason to account them strange. Let them be silent, and admire the works of God, whose ways are past finding out, and whose majesty is not confined to time, manner, or measure."

Many questioned why God would choose this wealthy landed gentleman to cure diseases in such an extraordinary manner. For Greatrakes, there was only one reason: to convince this "age of atheism, which many "pretended wits" have fallen into, of the truth of Jesus and Christianity. It was also to demonstrate the greatness of God's mercy that the Almighty would use such a worthless instrument as Greatrakes, mere dust and clay, to cure diseases that "no physick could move." Finally, he believed that God had chosen him in order "to abate the pride of the Papists" by demonstrating that God had chosen a Protestant "to do such strange things in the face of the sun, which they (the Catholics) pretend to do in cells." He would continue his argument, he writes, but declines, "lest I shall fall under the lash of unmerciful pens," for the "truth itself is sometimes better concealed than published."

Even Greatrakes' harshest critics found it difficult to disprove his power to heal. His most vehement detractor, David Lloyd, could not heap insults on him fast enough. Greatrakes was a "miracle monger," a "dreamer of dreams," and a "cheat" out to delude the population with "diabolical wonders." Yet the most that Lloyd could find to refute the healer's power was the proposition that these cures were accidental.

During the course of my work on Greatrakes, I told everyone I knew, and sometimes those I hardly knew, about the exciting project I was working on. No doubt at times my interest in this work got the best of me. My apologies to those who were more considerate in their patience than I was in my enthusiasm. This aside, it was always interesting to notice the reactions of people as I told them hard-to-swallow stories about Greatrakes. These stories elicited the whole gamut of reactions. Most interesting were those people who put up an immediate resistance. It was palpable. Their faces and eyes became fixed, masklike, perhaps because they were holding back from telling me how naive I was.

I do not know whether Greatrakes healed or not. The evidence, incredible to be sure, does suggest that something out of the ordinary was happening. Iain's view that our work was to uncover a lost piece of Anglo-Irish history is valid enough. And that in itself is intensely interesting. Here were real people—people of great note, no less—involved in a drama of grand proportions. Our approaching trip to England and Ireland was exciting in the extreme.

CHAPTER 3

*T*AIN AND I ARRIVED IN London late in the afternoon on
August 12, 1989, and settled into a hotel on Montague Street,
opposite the British Museum. While he went off to visit friends,
I set out for the rare book stores. My desire to find an original copy of
A Brief Account was working away at me. If a copy did exist, it seemed
that London would be the place to find it.

The atmosphere of a rare book store is entirely different from that
of a regular bookstore. Because prices tend to be higher and buyers
tend to have their well-chosen manias, there is an intensity underlying
the stores' apparent casualness. Buyers have particular interests and are
looking for specific items. The air is full of subtlety and desire. Someone
perusing a shelf with a look of complete distraction could underneath
be salivating in anticipation of a great find. In fact, wasn't that me?

When a clerk in a such a specialty bookstore approaches and asks, "Can I help you?" the last thing to say is, "Just looking." To be so unspecific, so indiscriminate, gains you no respect, and the clerk's smiling reply, "Please, do look around," will convey this message. It is always best to have something specific in mind when entering a rare book store. And the more obscure the better. The last thing you want to ask for is a title that the shop might actually have. If the staff does produce the book, you can't help but feel an obligation to buy it. The way out is to say, "Oh, I've already got that edition," or words to that effect. If you have a truly obscure title to ask for, as I did, all the better. Once the proprietor tells you the store hasn't got the book, you are released from any obligation and are free to browse.

Some collectors search for all the editions of a single title. Others will spend great sums of money on books they are not interested in but will purchase anyway because one book in the lot will complete a set. When I made the mistake of telling a well-known San Francisco book collector, the aforementioned psychiatrist who declared Greatrakes a paranoid schizophrenic, that I too was a collector, he was quick to correct me. "You're not a real book collector," he said. "Real collectors don't buy from passion; they buy for investment purposes."

Given my particular interest, I could enter any bookstore with complete confidence. "Can I help you, sir?" "Yes, I'm looking for a copy of *A Brief Account*, by Valentine Greatrakes and published in London in 1666." Often, clerks would react with an air of being caught up short, as if I had insulted them by asking for a title they had never heard of.

Invariably, they would consult with a colleague or check a list and then come back, half apologizing. "So sorry, we don't seem to have it." But I did find it, and in the most unexpected circumstances.

The next morning, Iain and I arose early and hurried down to the dining room of our B and B for breakfast. Is there anything more quaint and well intentioned than the dining room of a bed-and-breakfast? We stayed at many such inns during our travels, and whether they were on the high end or low end, they all reeked of the same atmosphere— well-kept tatter serving up eggs, bacon, fried tomatoes, toast with butter and marmalade, and all the coffee or tea you can drink.

At 9 AM, we were among the first in line to enter the British Museum. The British Library was still located inside the museum back in 1989. The library has since moved to newer, more modern quarters at Saint Pancras. Access to the library was carefully restricted. After a short interview by security, we were handed our photo ID cards, which are good for five years, and set to work. I never thought I would be so thrilled to walk into a library. But this was more than a library. This was a temple to the Western mind. I paused for a moment at the entrance to take everything in. The enormous circular room, with its large, domed skylight, had a grace and elegance long since eclipsed by the modern world. Long, wooden reading tables with leather tops were laid out fanlike around the room and were divided into numbered reading stations with folding book rests and individual reading lights. Nothing had changed here since the room opened in 1857. In the 1860s, Karl Marx sat at one of these tables, figuring out how to change the world.

Card catalogs were nowhere in sight, not because they had been replaced by computers, but because the library operated on an even older system. Instead, the library's vast holdings were listed in large volumes resembling oversized photo albums with rigid covers. Within these tomes, many of the book titles were handwritten in nineteenth-century script, or else typed on small pieces of paper and then pasted onto the page. Scouring the pages of these large volumes, one cannot fail to be impressed by the sheer amount of material collected over the centuries. It is tremendously reassuring to be in a place where our history is so revered and such care is taken toward its preservation.

While the books of the British Library were held in the round reading room, the handwritten documents, correspondence, and so forth were in the Manuscript Room in another section of the museum. To get there, one walked through several large halls whose glass cases displayed various historical documents: the Magna Carta, an original page of Emily Brontë, and a page by Charles Dickens, for example. One case displayed the lyrics of a Beatles song hastily written by Paul McCartney on a piece of paper. In years to come, will today's great writers be represented by the original computer disc on which they wrote their works?

Iain and I staked out a table for ourselves and, for the next three days, piled it high with books. With all of British history at our fingertips, we could not call up books fast enough. Among the many things we found were Greatrakes' original account books for the years 1663 to 1679. On May 14, 1675, he acquired five new milk cows. One has the impression that in the seventeenth century, people were running all over Great Britain collecting any scrap of paper with anything written on it. A surprising find was that Greatrakes had dined with William Penn in 1670. But perhaps the most unlikely encounter occurred during the summer of 1665, when Greatrakes met Prince Rupert, nephew of King Charles I. This incident must have been thick with meaning.

During the English civil war, Rupert led the Royalist forces with bold and daring passion against Cromwell's parliamentary army. Not only did Rupert live through the monarchy's defeat, but he also watched helplessly as his uncle was beheaded in public. The prince must have known that Greatrakes had served in Cromwell's army, and it is difficult to imagine that Rupert would have had much sympathy for old Cromwellians. Yet in a letter from Henry Oldenburg to Robert Boyle, we learned that Greatrakes was in Rupert's house to treat a friend for terrible backaches after the prince "argued him to suffer that friction."

The meeting reveals Greatrakes' success at repositioning himself to the restored Crown. Stubbe's book about Greatrakes, in fact, speaks directly to this point. The title, *The Miraculous Conformist*, means just that—one who has miraculously conformed to the reestablished Crown.

On our first night in London, Iain and I sat in a pub studying maps of England and Ireland and plotting our itinerary. The land, the land. I wanted to see the Greatrakes land. I had no idea what I would find, but I wanted to go there. We went over the list of places to visit, figured the distances, assessed the time needed at each place, and so on. Then Iain said, "How is it we never thought of going to Ragley?" This caught me short. Ragley, of course . . . why hadn't we thought of that? Did it still exist? "A couple of phone calls, and we'll know," he said.

The next morning, Iain was on the phone. "Hello! Is this the Marquis? . . . Good morning to you, sir!" Ragley did exist and was owned today by the Marquis of Hertford, a descendent of the Conways. Iain mentioned Greatrakes, but got little response. Apparently, the marquis did not know who Greatrakes was. Iain told him of our project and that we'd like to visit, but this, too, elicited little reaction.

Thinking on his feet, Iain then said, "We're making a movie!" (Well, we did think this would make a great movie.) That changed everything. "Yes, yes!" the Marquis exclaimed. "I'd love to see you. Do come around when you're in the area! Love to see you." Iain filled me in on the recent history of the English nobility. "They're basically paupers living the sham life of the rich. They've got huge properties and houses that they can barely maintain and will do anything to bring in money. The prospect of Ragley being used as a movie location is certain to induce the salivating response." This would be our first stop out of London.

The next morning, I worked in the British Library while Iain went to work at the Royal Society. This is the same Royal Society cofounded by Robert Boyle in 1660. Later in the afternoon, I taxied over to meet him. The library of the Royal Society is only a fraction of the size of the British Library, but with a more personal atmosphere, like the private library of a very wealthy friend. I found Iain seated at a table in the corner with a large binder. He looked up at me with a broad smile. "Hello, Leonard," he said, gesturing toward the book. "I'd like you to meet Mr. Greatrakes." At the bottom of the page, I saw the signature in florid script—Valentine Greatrakes. Here was an actual letter written by Greatrakes to Robert Boyle in 1668.

The wish of anyone reconstructing the life of a figure from the past is to spend an evening with one's subject, not only to ply the person with questions, but also to get a feel for who he or she was as a person. Short of that, one gleans every scrap of information one can find, to put muscle and sinew onto the skeleton of mere facts. Sitting with an actual letter written by the person brings that presence closer.

Greatrakes wrote the letter while at the English port of Minehead on his way home after his second trip to England. He had visited with Boyle a few days earlier. Were it not for this letter, we would not have known that Greatrakes ever made a second trip abroad. In his letter to Boyle, Greatrakes tells of visiting the Conways again, as well as some people he had cured two years earlier. These are not the actions of a mountebank. Greatrakes also describes a number of cures he performed during these travels, thus contradicting his detractors' stories that after his first trip to England his powers flamed out and he fell into obscurity.

Robert Boyle

With no mention of this visit to England anywhere in correspondence or newspapers of the period, we can only assume that Greatrakes was not the center of notoriety as he had been in the past. Yet he was still attacked by those trying to undermine him. In his letter, he writes that he has "but one thing to beg and desire" of his friend Boyle. If anyone can prove that any of the cures he claims to have performed are false, then "publish me to the world to be a liar and impostor." Wearied of the fray and longing to return home, Greatrakes writes that he would never "live in a city to lose the happiness of my innocent country life."

While facing his detractors, Greatrakes always maintained an appearance of composure and self-confidence. Inwardly, though, he was racked with self-doubt. Even he wondered about his healing power. Were the cures due to the patient's imagination or rather to an innate power he carried within himself? In his doubt, he questioned whether his talent was "a temptation and delusion of Satan" or an ability that came to him from God. But, in 1665, something truly strange happened.

Neo-Platonist philosopher Joseph Glanvill wrote of Greatrakes' self-doubt. One night, as Greatrakes lay in bed, "one of his hands was struck dead," and the impulse came to him to try his power on himself, which he did, "stroking [his deadened hand] with his other hand, and then it immediately returned to its former liveliness. This was repeated two or three nights." We read about the same episode in a letter by a Dublin minister: "It was said to him, that his right arm should be smitten and withered for his [lack of] belief and that by rubbing it with his left it should be well again, which accordingly came to pass." More than any other experience, this episode convinced Greatrakes that his gift of healing was "an extraordinary gift of God."

If Iain and I had ever doubted the value of making this trip to London, our finds at the Royal Society and the British Library set our minds straight. Along with the Minehead letter, we found a copy of Stubbe's book, *The Miraculous Conformist.* I had first seen a copy at Stanford some months earlier, but this copy at the British Library contained something truly extraordinary. I was going through some old journals when the book was delivered to our reading station. Iain began paging through it and actually exclaimed—that is, he exclaimed as loudly as one can in the British Library, "Good Lord! Leonard, this is it!" I leaned over to take a look. In the margin of the book was a note written in an anonymous, seventeenth-century hand: "H. Stubbe told me he writt this booke as a snare in hope some of the clergy would write against him."

A puzzle that had been bothering us for months was now solved. Early in our research, Iain questioned why Stubbe would go to the trouble to write a book about Greatrakes, and in such haste. *The Miraculous Conformist* was published in January 1666, only a few weeks after Stubbe saw Greatrakes at the Conway estate at Ragley. Others had witnessed the same cures and were just as impressed, but only Stubbe took the pains to rush out and write a book. What prompted him to take such quick action?

With this note in the margin, everything fell into place. The answer was Stubbe's radicalism. When the Crown was restored in 1660, Stubbe was forced to bury his antimonarchist sentiments. By 1666, he was tired of living in the shadows, playing the role of the good little Royalist. More than anything else, he wanted an opportunity to get back into the public eye. Greatrakes provided just that opportunity. Stubbe knew that the dangerous implications of Greatrakes' cures would rattle both church and state, and that the controversy that was sure to follow would return Stubbe to the spotlight.

He also knew that his book would find a much wider audience if he could attach to it the illustrious name of Robert Boyle, and so he mentions Boyle on the title page of the book. *The Miraculous Conformist*, it turns out, is a clever piece of manipulation whereby Stubbe uses both Boyle and Greatrakes as foils to further his own agenda. Stubbe and Boyle had crossed paths before, and while they were not the worst of enemies, they were clearly on the opposite sides of many important issues. A few years later, as Stubbe gained confidence in wielding his incendiary pen, he became one of the harshest critics of Boyle's beloved Royal Society. Stubbe even took payment from a member of the College of Physicians to keep up his steady stream of invective against the society.

Boyle had heard the stories of Greatrakes' cures from colleagues, but never having witnessed the healer, he refused to offer an opinion. Henry Oldenburg, the first secretary of the Royal Society, wrote Boyle in the summer of 1665, questioning his reticence to accept the reports of cures.

> I find, Sir, by your silence that you are not satisfied with the testimonials hitherto given of the Irish healer. Dr. Beale and Dr. Sydenham jump in a full assurance of the truth of the thing. [Sydenham] brought as much prejudice against [Greatrakes] as any man could, but now has no more reason to doubt it, than to doubt whether he is a man, or some other animal.

Another letter from Oldenburg followed several weeks later. It was an account of a child suffering "with horrid pain" from "the stone, or other stoppage of urine." After being treated by Greatrakes, the child was "perfectly natural and without pain."

When Boyle saw Stubbe's book in March 1666, he went livid. He was at his manor in Stalbridge, preparing to leave the next morning on a journey of several days, when the book arrived late at night by express mail.

Boyle's friend Daniel Coxe had seen the book at the printer's shop in London while it was still in production. Noticing Boyle's name on the title page, he recognized immediately that his friend was being dragged into an affair he knew nothing about. He sent Boyle a copy of the book posthaste. Boyle's hair must have stood on end when he saw Stubbe's writing. The intelligentsia, Boyle feared, would assume he knew Greatrakes' work and would therefore expect him to have an opinion on the man. What was even more risky, they would assume that Boyle was partisan to the dangerous religious implications of the healings.

Boyle's initial reaction grew worse as he read the book. Stubbe's interpretation of Greatrakes' healing power, calculated to shock, had all the desired effect. Boyle picked up his pen and stayed up the whole night, firing off a lengthy reply to Stubbe. The formality of the language lends an almost stylized quality to his anger.

> I must confess to you that I did not see the manuscript before it came abroad. For if I had seen what you wrote about miracles, I should freely have dissuaded you from publicly addressing to me, what I cannot but much dissent from; and perhaps I should have been able to prevail with you to omit all that part of your epistle.

Beneath the polite form, Boyle was seething. Stubbe believed that Greatrakes' cures were miracles, a dangerous belief indeed. Were this true, Boyle replied, it would "degrade the unquestionable miraculous gifts of the apostles" and reduce them to the level of Greatrakes. Boyle criticized Stubbe for his failure to distinguish between the natural and the miraculous. Mixing the two degraded the truly supernatural miracles of Christ and the apostles. Boyle was willing to admit that there might be an element of the miraculous in Greatrakes' healings, but insisted his "gift" should be looked on "as a distinct and inferior kind [of power rather] than degrade the unquestionable gifts of the apostles." According to Boyle, a true miracle was an event that overrode the laws of the physical world. Without having seen Greatrakes' cures, he was certain there had to be a physical basis to them.

Stubbe agreed with Greatrakes that his ability to heal was a gift of God and that the curing itself was brought about by the healing power of nature. "It is nature [that] cures the diseases," Stubbe wrote. "We are but servants to nature, to remove impediments, or strengthen her that she may effect the work." This was an odious thought to Boyle. Human beings could never be subservient to nature. Following Genesis, he believed in a Divine-given hierarchy in which humans sat at the apex of the natural world. Nature serves man, not the reverse. It was this hierarchy that underlay what Boyle termed the "Empire of Man over the inferior creatures of God." Any "veneration" for the natural world was in his view only a "discouraging impediment" to this domination.

Remarkably, Boyle bent over backward to offer Stubbe an out for his disturbing ideas. Boyle even went as far as suggesting that perhaps the reason for Stubbe's "unstudied expressions" was because the writer was in such a hurry to publish his book. Moreover, Boyle told Stubbe that he would not take Stubbe's ideas as "deliberate tenets" unless Stubbe were to "surprise" Boyle by declaring them to be so. What proof of Stubbe's seriousness did Boyle need, beyond Stubbe's publication of these very ideas?

Boyle reminded Stubbe of the problems the writer had encountered in the past because of his "meddling with theological matters" and warned Stubbe that the book's interpretation of Greatrakes' cures would surely bring the author more trouble. Stubbe could not have cared less. As he had hoped, news of his book traveled fast. In a matter of days of its going on sale, the philosopher Henry More wrote his friend Anne Conway, telling her about the book and the "resentment of serious men . . . For they look upon his management of the matter not so advantageous for religion." Stubbe could not have been more pleased. Boyle was cornered, and the scientist knew it. He had no choice now but to seek out Greatrakes, to observe him at work firsthand, to formulate his own opinion. When he learned that Greatrakes was in London, Boyle made immediate plans to go there.

In preparation for his trip, Boyle composed a list of seventeen points that would serve as a basis for investigation. We uncovered this list during our first day at the British Library. It provides a fascinating picture of the intersection of the new scientific method and older beliefs about health and human functioning.

1. What is his constitution? Is he melancholy, sanguine, phlegmatic and C [choleric]. What diseases has he suffered from? Is he fat, lean, vigorous, weak? What is his age?

2. When did he first have the impulse to cure? Was this preceded by any sickness, melancholy, or an accident that might have any extraordinary influence upon his mind?

3. Before he cures does he perform any ceremony using words or prayer? Are they arbitrary words or some set form? If the latter, what is it? Does he require the patient to do or say anything before and after he has stroked?

4. Does he apply his hands only slightly to the affected part, or must he rub it also, and if friction is necessary, must it be light or strong, and how long must it continue?

5. Can he perform cures and remove pains when the patient is clothed or whether immediate contact is necessary?

6. Do his left hand and right hand stroke with equal efficacy; and whether the contact of his cheek and breast can equal that of his hand?

7. Are his gloves, shirt, and stockings that have just been worn upon his flesh of equal efficacy as his hand in the cure of diseases, or at least in the removing of pain? How long will their efficacy last after his ceasing to wear them? Will the degrees or duration of their virtue increase if they are taken from his body when he is sweating, or at least more than ordinary warm?

8. What is the efficacy of his spittle, and his urine, and if they have any, how long will it last?

9. Is his urine more effective when warm or cold? Will its

sanative virtue be preserved longer if it [be] kept close stopped, and whether a little spot of salt, or nitre, etc, dropped into it, while it is yet fresh and sanative, will change the texture and destroy or impair the virtue? If unaltered will his urine retain a sanative virtue?

10. What are the diseases that Mr. G. cannot at all cure? Among those which he sometimes cures, which are they that he succeeds best, and which he succeeds worst with? Among the former, what complexions, ages, sexes, etc, do the most favor, or disfavor his cures?

11. Upon his touching, or stroking does there ensue at any time, any quick and manifest evacuation of matter by vomit, siege, sweat, urine, or salivation?

12. Will his sanative power react to the curing or removing pains in horses, dogs, or other brutes?

13. Is it true that the effluvia of his body are well scented, when he has employed no proper means to make it so?

14. Can he cure any possessed person, or any disease (if there be any such) produced by witchcraft?

15. Can he cure men of different religions as Roman Catholics, Socinians, Jews, etc, as well as infants, or distracted persons to whose recovery the faith of the patient cannot concur?

16. How many times must he touch the patients, and at what intervals between those times?

17. Is the efficacy or inefficacy of his touch always proportional to the greater or lesser danger, or obstinacy of the malady, considered as physicians are want to estimate it?

While we do not know how Greatrakes measured up to Boyle's long list of questions, we do know that Boyle became one of his most ardent supporters and signed his name to seven affidavits as an eyewitness.

Further proof that Boyle was more than just a passing witness to the cures was a letter we found in the Manuscript Room of the British Library. The letter was dated Easter Sunday, 1666. Writing to an unknown correspondent, Boyle describes an evening he spent with Greatrakes at the apartment of Boyle's sister, Lady Ranelagh, in London, along with a number of cures he saw Greatrakes perform there.

In Boyle's own hand, he writes of observing Greatrakes cure a young woman of deafness by having only "put his fingers in her ears, and (as I remember) a little stroked them." When the woman then felt a great pain in her forehead, he stroked her there. She felt the pain move "from place to place about her head" until both the pain and the deafness were gone. When Boyle asked the woman how long she had been "thick of hearing," she answered ever since the birth of her first child about a year and a quarter ago. Affirming she was recovered, "she went away joyful."

But there were stranger things yet. Boyle writes about the sister's servant, who suffered from a "tedious and violent fit of the headache." Without actually touching her head, Greatrakes laid his hand on her hood and stroked her. The pain was gone, but she then felt a giddiness and trembling. He stroked the "middle of her head without taking off her hood," after which she felt fine and went on her way, "leaving Mr. G to resume his discourse, which he pursued as unconcernedly as if nothing had happened at all to interrupt it."

Like other pieces of correspondence we found, Boyle's letter had never been transcribed, and thus it was left to Iain and me to sit in the Manuscript Room, trying to decipher those seventeenth-century letters into modern English. To avoid losing valuable time, we obtained copies of the letters so that we could work on them in California at a more leisurely pace. Because of Iain's work schedule, the task of transcribing these letters fell to me. I had no knowledge of the phrasing and termi-nology of earlier English, nor any understanding of the abbreviations that were commonly used to make writing easier. I discovered much of this as I went along.

For example: the *th* of many words was commonly transposed to a *y*. Thus, in Greatrakes' time, the word *them* was written "ym." The word *that* was written "yt" and *the* becomes "ye." This means that the term *ye*, as in "ye olde," which Americans are so fond of saying when trying to evoke olden times, was never spoken, but only written.

"This bad weather & long nights, would indeed keep mee close to my studyes, were I happy in eyes, yt would bare reading; but I am too sensible of ye weaknesse of ym, and therefore lay asyde all bookes at candle lighting: So yt having so much necessary businesse upon mee by preaching twice in a week, besydes ye diversions of visits, & riding out sometimes for health sake. [illegible text] I am forced to be slower in my answeres then I would otherwise be." —Opening paragraph of Cambridge University Letter as deciphered by Leonard Pitt

Adding to the difficulty of transcribing, handwriting itself was different in those days. A seventeenth-century *h* is very different from the *h* of today. Because the language was not standardized, a single word would often be spelled differently within the same document. The task of deciphering these manuscripts was both fascinating and dreadful. At times, I spent a whole day on only two or three words, taking them apart letter by letter, to make endless comparisons with other words.

One day, Iain happened by while I was struggling with a particularly recalcitrant word. Hours of wrestling, trying every possible combination, had led nowhere. I was at wit's end. Context is a key in transcribing old manuscripts, but even this didn't work here. While we pored over the text, trying everything to solve the riddle, a friend of mine stopped by. She looked carefully at the paper and said, "Hmm, looks like *Vespasian*, doesn't it?" Iain and I were dumbfounded. She was right. It was a name; that's what had confused us. Vespasian, the Roman emperor!

While Iain and I managed to accommodate ourselves to the unreality of Greatrakes' history, the constant challenge of reading reports of cures that were too strange to be true yet too substantiated to be false was sometimes almost too much to take. It was like viewing a hologram that has all the detail and dimension of a real object yet will disappear in an instant when seen from a particular angle. I could not help but think that if I could only get the right perspective, the right vantage point, I would be able to truly understand what was before me. But if I did so, perhaps that understanding, too, would disappear. Or perhaps not.

What actually took place during one of Greatrakes' healing sessions? His stroking varied greatly from person to person. Some patients were stroked vigorously for as long as an hour and felt better. Others were cured after only a brief and light stroking. A number of those he treated showed signs of improvement but then relapsed. Many received no benefit at all. Others had immediate success, throwing away their crutches and leaping about, and remained well. Some reported that his hands were very warm, that "the bath never heated up as did the hand of Mr. Greatericks." Others reported that his hand was cold, yet still did "produce such a heat as did burn up all the pain."

One could find some rationale to explain certain of the cures: His talent might have lain in an ability to move energy through the body, something akin to acupressure. The sore, the tumor, the paralysis, was only a symptom. He treated the condition on the underlying level of energy. Move the energy in the body, restore the energy flow, and the condition changes for the better. Maybe Greatrakes was performing a primitive kind of accupressure, working with pressure points in order to move energy through the body. A handy explanation that says little.

But any level of comfort we achieved around the cures vanished quickly with reports of even stranger cures. When treating the king's evil, Greatrakes would ask the patient to apply a daily poultice of boiled turnips. This was a typical treatment of the day and was most likely something he learned from his wife. But what about the cases in which he would lance a tumor and "squeeze out the cores and corruption, and in a few days it would be well with his only stroking it every morning"? Greatrakes performed such an operation on Doctor Ralph Cudworth's little boy, who suffered from tumors in his chest. The healer opened the tumors to "let out the corrupt matter, and since the sores are healed and the wounds dried up." Cudworth was a noted philosopher and scholar and, along with Henry More, was one of the foremost figures among the Cambridge Platonists.

Or stranger yet: When treating ulcers or running sores, Greatrakes used his saliva on his hand or finger. He also used saliva in treating deafness. In the case of a Mrs. Lile, "he put some of his spittle into her ears and turning his finger in her ears, rubbed and chafed them well, which cured her both of the pain & deafness." In the case of a young boy cured of leprosy, Greatrakes "rubbed his body all over with his spittle."

What is to be made of reports that Greatrakes' urine smelled of violets and had a powerful curative effect? Elenor Dickinson was nearly deaf and went to Greatrakes' house in London, but because of the large crowds, she could not get near him. So she "snatched some of his urine, and drank it." She also put some into her ears "and immediately heard the noise around her." Several hours later, "she voided nearly four gallons of water, with a great quantity of wind." Her belly, which had been two yards around, shrunk to three-quarters of a yard. She also testified to having vomited out "several pieces of thick skin drawn over with blue veins." She now "confesses herself to be perfectly cured."

Could there be anything stranger? Yes. In one cure recorded by Doctor Fairclough, Greatrakes took off his leather glove, turned it inside out, and gave it to Robert Boyle, who then passed it over the body of the noted tinker Robert Furnace "and so proceeded to pursue his pains from place to place, until they fled quite out at the ends of the toes." If his glove had a curative power, Greatrakes wondered, perhaps his shirt would, too. He took it off, rubbed it on Furnace's chest, and tried to cure him, but to no effect.

Once more, Iain and I came back to the question of belief. Were people cured because they believed that Greatrakes could heal? But events contradicted us. On his way to Ragley in January 1666, Greatrakes stopped for the night in a house in Warwickshire. One of the gentlemen lodging there suffered from poor sight in one eye and, even though he had heard stories of Greatrakes' stupendous cures, was a thorough nonbeliever. The women of the house encouraged the afflicted man to let Greatrakes treat him, but the gentleman "made very dainty of it." Greatrakes, for his part, said that he would not touch anyone who did not want to be touched. But the women insisted, and after much urging, both men agreed "the one to touch, the other to be touched." After being stroked on his eye, the man declared that he saw much more clearly than before. Afterward, he complained of "a pain and heaviness in his head … upon a new application of Mr. Greataricks' hand, he said his pain was now gone." Another skeptic who finally submitted to Greatrakes' stroking ended his affidavit by saying that whatever credit he must give to others who have helped him, "I must double upon Greatrakes."

Maybe Greatrakes was a master hypnotist and cured by delusion. Maybe he tricked his patients into getting well. Perhaps he excited people's imagination to such a degree that they healed themselves. Is this method of healing illegitimate because it is unorthodox? What would the healed person say? The age-old question of the mind-body connection comes into play here. To what degree can mental suggestion alter a person's physical state?

CHAPTER 4

A T THE END OF OUR STAY in London, Iain and I drove out of the city at breakneck speed and headed for Ragley. Because I could not tolerate driving on the left side of the road, Iain did all the driving. One of the great luxuries of traveling on a project like this is the total absence of distractions. No mail, no phone calls, no shopping, no demands of any kind. Only the work. Our time on the road was particularly fruitful. Working in libraries was continually frustrating: racing against the clock to order books before the last call, the long lines in the photocopy room, waiting for some slowpoke to finish so that I could photocopy crucial pages. But the road was complete freedom, a time for connecting the dots in order to see the big picture.

The short monographs we found on Greatrakes usually covered the same fare: how he came to healing, accounts of cures, and so forth.

None of these writings mentioned that shortly before he began healing, Greatrakes was involved in one of the few witch trials to be held in Ireland, where he acted as an amateur witch finder. No one mentioned, either, that behind the facade of his toe-the-line Church of England Protestantism lay a religious radical. Find the dots and connect them. While driving to Ragley we did just that.

A particular set of dots came to us through a nineteenth-century version of the Internet. Known as *Notes and Queries*, the publication began in 1849 and was miraculously still in existence, at least in the mid-1990s. Anyone seeking information on any subject, be it historical, literary, or genealogical, writes a query letter to the publication and then waits for a reader to answer in a future issue. There are no articles per se, only letters from people seeking or offering information. Nothing is too obscure: "Can any of your readers inform me why the five crosses forming the present Jerusalem cross were adopted as symbolic of the Holy Land?" Or, "I should be much obliged if I could obtain information on the following battles fought in England."

In May 1864, an inquiry about Greatrakes appeared, requesting information on the English branch of the family. Two weeks later, a reader answered, referring the correspondent to an elaborate genealogy compiled by the Rev. Samuel Hayman, "the historian of Youghal." Hayman was a collateral descendant of Greatrakes and, like many retired Irish clerics, spent his time unearthing his family's history. We did find the genealogy, whose meticulous detail became one of the keys to our work.

But it was in June 1864 that a startling entry appeared in *Notes and Queries*. On his way to the Conway estate in January 1666, Greatrakes stopped in the city of Worcester and performed a number of cures there. About a month later, just as he was about to return to Ireland, a messenger arrived from Worcester extending an invitation to Greatrakes from the mayor and aldermen of the city to attend a celebration there in his honor. Greatrakes accepted.

This letter, dated 1864, contained, of all things, the original budget from the Worcester archives, detailing the expenses spent by the city on this celebration. In this simple yet extraordinary document entitled "The Charge of Entertainment for Mr. Gratix," dated 1666, we learned that the entertainment took place at a Mr. Wythie's house, who received £5. The man who went to fetch Greatrakes, a Mr. Nicolas Baker, received 15 shillings for his trouble. The wine served at the entertainment was provided by Messrs. Read and Solley at a cost of £1, 10 shillings, 10 pence. The cider was provided by a Mr. William Tompkins for 3 shillings, 10 pence. Greatrakes traveled with an assistant, whose "man" received 5 shillings.

A note at the bottom of the article read "This was an Irishman, famous for helping and curing many lame and diseased people . . . and therefore sent for to this and many other places."

One of the first people Greatrakes met when he arrived in Worcester on Monday, February 12, 1666, was John Flamsteed, the future Astronomer Royal. Flamsteed had visited Greatrakes in Affane in 1665, when the healer had stroked him in an attempt to cure a rheumatic condition he had suffered from since childhood, but Flamsteed received no benefit. In Worcester he was stroked again, but his condition persisted. Despite his disappointment, Flamsteed wrote of having seen others cured. By this time, Greatrakes' curing powers were so well known that a number of eminent physicians were studying him closely, observing his cures and recording the results. One such observer, E. Foxcroft, a fellow of King's College, Cambridge, had been with Greatrakes at Ragley and accompanied him to Worcester to record the treatments, the failures as well as the successes, that occurred there. At Stubbe's request, Foxcroft's account was included in *The Miraculous Conformist*.

Several days after Greatrakes' arrival in Worcester—February 15, to be exact—a messenger arrived from London with a summons from the king ordering Greatrakes to the capital at once. The king wanted to witness the stupendous cures he had heard so much about. The urgency of the demand was underscored by the identity of the king's emissary to Worcester. He was none other than Lord Arlington, the English minister of state and the second most important man in King Charles II's inner circle. Some say that Arlington's name is part of the origin of the word *cabal*, which is purportedly an acronym comprising the names Clifford, Ashley, Buckingham, Arlington, and Lauderdale—all members of Charles' inner circle.

What must Greatrakes have thought, to be summoned to London by the king himself and to be notified by an emissary as important as Arlington? In a letter to Edward Conway, Greatrakes wrote that he actually welcomed the interruption, for he was "glad to be freed" from the great crowds at Worcester, "where I was like to be bruised to death." Little did he know what was in store for him.

Greatrakes arrived in London in February 1666 and settled into lodgings in the Lincoln's Inn Fields district of the city. London's population then stood at no more than half a million. Fifty years later, these numbers would nearly double. With the city growing at this rate, it was difficult to know when one actually entered the capital. A sure sign was when one's coach left the dirt roads and "was got upon the stones." The cobblestones brought not only the certainty of having arrived at the center of the English civilized world, but also a great deal of noise. The sound of iron and wooden wheels clanging and clattering along the city thoroughfares was deafening. Add to this the hawkers with their cries—the custard mongers, tinkers, milkmaids, and water carriers—and the din increased. The narrow streets of the city were choked with carriages, coaches, and carts of all sorts, which created one great, heaping traffic mess. The drivers sitting in their open vehicles shouted and barked at one another as they tried to undo the confusion. Walking in front of the nobleman's coach was the footman, bellowing out for the commoners to make way, a call often answered by jeers and ridicule.

Along with the cobblestones to announce one's arrival into the capital, there was also the intense barrage of smells wafting from every part of the city. Down the center of each street ran an open sewer carrying human waste poured by the bucketful from the houses every morning.

Many of these putrid odors were trapped in the air by the dense clouds of smoke and vapor that spewed from the smokestacks of the brewers, dyers, and soap-boilers who carried on their manufacturing in the heart of the city. John Evelyn, the indefatigable diarist of seventeenth-century London, complained of the oppressive smoke, "which fouls our clothes and corrupts the waters."

Street illumination by lantern at night was scant and was found only on the city's main thoroughfares. The mazes of narrow, crooked side streets were unlit and often dangerous places to negotiate on foot in the dark. Standing at street corners were homeless boys equipped with torch and lantern. Known as link boys, these urchins were willing to light anyone's way for a few pennies.

The real life of London, though, was found on its main artery, the River Thames. Stretching for eight miles, the Thames was the main thoroughfare for travelers making use of a multitude of boat taxis—tilt-boats, tide boats, and wherries, all ferrying passengers from one end of the city to the other, thus avoiding the noise, discomfort, and delays of traveling along congested and bumpy city streets. Also on the river were great numbers of long, shallow boats used for the transport of goods—hay, straw, coal, beans, wood, and so forth—to supply the city's endless appetite. Add to this the gilded barges of the king and other nobility, plus the private yachts of the wealthy, and the nautical picture was complete.

During the severest of winters, when the river froze over and became a solid mass of ice, the watery thoroughfare became the site of the ice fair. People walked, skated, and rode in coaches on the ice, enjoying themselves at the various attractions—puppet shows, bullbaiting, horse races—and stopped at the many food stalls along the way. In October, the annual water procession took place amid much pomp and fanfare as the newly elected lord mayor of London and his entourage stepped aboard their decorated barges and, to the salute of cannon fire, sailed from London to Westminster to be received by the king. The Thames had no embankment then, and the houses came right down to the river's edge, providing a fine vantage point for spectators looking out on the festivities from windows, stairs, and gardens.

When Greatrakes arrived in London, the city was just emerging from the ravages of the Great Plague. The last time the disease had stalked the city was in 1630. Fears that the cataclysm might strike again surfaced in September 1664, when news reached the capital that the plague had struck Holland and was devastating Amsterdam and Rotterdam. The weeks passed, and the island nation appeared safe from the infection. Then, around early December, two Frenchmen in London's Drury Lane died of the disease. The plague had found its way to England yet again.

The plague attacks the lymphatic glands, particularly in the groin, armpit, and throat, which swell and present what was commonly called the plague bubo. Abscesses develop, and highly virulent pus is discharged. Patients sometimes recovered. Those who did not died from blood poisoning. Through the winter and spring of 1664–1665, the disease was confined mainly to the western section of the city, felling

*Mortality Bill listing diseases and casualty rates in London for
the week of August 15–22, 1665. Plague deaths: 4,237.*

relatively small numbers of people. Each week, the city posted the
Mortality Bill, which listed the total number of deaths in London, with
a breakdown according to the cause of death. City officials reduced the
numbers by attributing some plague deaths to "spotted fever" or some
other disease so as not to alarm the populace.

By mid-June, close to one hundred people were dying of the dis-
ease every week. By September, this number had climbed to upward of

one thousand a day. Church bells tolled throughout the city, sounding out their requiems. Empty streets echoed to the cry "Bring out your dead!"

At the first real signs of the pestilence in June, the king and his court fled to Oxford. A steady stream of carriages and carts followed the monarch, carrying off the nobility and gentry to the safety of their country homes. As thousands fled the city, shops closed and tradespeople lost their employment. It was not known then that the source of the misery was a bacillus transmitted to humans by fleas riding on infected rats and other rodents. This ignorance generated rampant fears about how people contracted the disease. Everyone avoided physical contact at all costs. At the market, the butcher would let the customers take a joint of meat off the hook themselves rather than hand it to them. Vendors would not take money directly from customers, but had them put it into a pot of vinegar. Customers carried coins for small change, so that they would not have to take change in return. Many thought the plague was due to contaminated air and lit bonfires in the streets as a purifier. Fearful that infected air could escape from plague-ridden houses, people walked down the middle of the street so as to avoid doorways.

Those people who were found infected with the disease were locked up in their houses, along with everyone else in the household. A guard was posted at the door to stop anyone from entering or leaving and to see that all necessities were delivered to those held inside. A large red cross was painted on the doorway with the words "Lord, have mercy on us." Passersby could hear mournful cries from inside as people died an agonizing death or suffered the pain of watching their loved ones sicken and die.

Large pits were dug and filled with thousands of corpses, which were hauled to the site on horse-drawn dead-carts led by men purposely made drunk to render them capable of carrying out their gruesome task. Some of the infected, in a raving and delirious state, threw themselves into the pits and tried to bury themselves. Others stumbled to the edge and keeled over, dead.

The streets of London were plastered with handbills advertising every sort of miracle concoction to ward off the plague: "Infallible Preventive Pills Against the Plague," or "Never-Failing Preservatives Against the Infection" and "Incomparable Drink Against the Plague, Never Found Out Before." Shrewd hawkers made a handy profit by selling charms, potions, and amulets, all guaranteed to protect against the disease. The plague peaked in September, when over twenty-five thousand people had died of the disease. By early March 1666, the worst was over, and Charles and his court returned to the capital.

As literacy and cheap printing became more widespread in the seventeenth century, there was a proliferation of handbills and broadsides advertising the remedies, potions, nostrums, elixirs, and pills of doctors and quacks, apothecaries, astrologers, and anyone else purporting to cure humanity's ills. One of the more successful quacks of the period, Doctor John Case, illustrates the milieu of the period. Case came to London to seek his fortune at about age fifteen. By his midtwenties, he had published two books and gained a reputation as a medical writer.

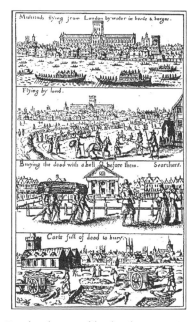

London decimated by the plague in 1665

Over the door of his house at Black-Friers, he had inscribed, "Within this place lives Doctor Case." A contemporary of his noted, "Case made more money by this couplet, than Dryden made by all his poetical works put together."

One night at dinner, a colleague of Case's, Doctor Radcliffe, made a toast: "Here's to all the fools, your [patients], brother Case!" To which Case replied, "I thank you good brother. Let me have all the fools and you are heartily welcome to the rest of the practise."

Case's mentor was another famed quack, Thomas Saffold, who never charged for his advice, on the condition that the patient bought a bottle of his elixir or a box of his famous pills. Saffold was well aware of the persuasive power of advertising and employed hired hands to walk the streets of London, distributing his poetic handbills. "It's Saffold's pills much better than the rest, deservedly have gained the name of best." Scurvy, French pox, agues, stone, and gout were all diseases to be cured by Saffold's remarkable pills. Any failure of the remedy to work its magic was handily explained by invoking God's will. "[Saffold] can cure when God Almighty pleases, but cannot protect against diseases. If men will live intemperate and sin, he cannot help it if they be sick again."

Another famous quack of the period, James Tilburg, made the claim that he could help married men who have "lost their nature." His cure alone "cherishes up the saddened spirits of the married man and does quicken them as a rose that hath received the summer's dew."

It was into this uncertain world of hope, fear, and expectation that Greatrakes arrived. The stories of cures that preceded him in the press or by rumor created a furor of anticipation. Reports that he had been summoned to the capital by the king would only intensify the news of Greatrakes' arrival.

On March 3, only a few days after Greatrakes reached the capital, the royal physicians ordered him to treat the courtier-poet Sir John Denham. The cure did not go well. It is not known what Denham suffered from; he had earlier been treated in Holland, where he took "fluxing pills," which did him no good at all. Subsequently, the doctors rubbed his shins with mercury. It was believed that this caused a nerve condition that was made worse by the "rough stroking of Greatrakes upon his limbs." Denham ended up going mad. On March 15, a note in the state papers reported that "People flock after Greatres still, but several who have been stroked by him decry him." The Greatrakes issue, though, was far from being settled.

On April 24, Greatrakes was put to another test. This time, the royal physician John Micklethwaite presented him with three chronically ill patients from Saint Bartholomew's Hospital. Later that day, Greatrakes wrote to Edward Conway describing the experience: "The King's doctors this day (for the confirmation of their Majesties belief) sent three out of the hospital to me who came on crutches, and blessed be God, they all went home well, to the admiration of all people, as well as the doctors."

The cures of these people are presented in *A Brief Account* with names of eyewitnesses. The first patient, a seaman, Joseph Warden, age forty-five, walked on crutches because of a violent pain in his leg. He was stroked until "he who came on his crutches, walked up and down very lustily without them, and so departed, resolving speedily to return to his ship."

The second patient, William Levell, a twenty-four-year-old cook, had been hospitalized for ten months at Saint Bartholomew's with a pain in his hip and knee. The pain was stroked out of his body through his toes, and "he confessed himself to be in perfect ease."

The third patient, Francis Steele, sixty-three, had been disabled for six months and was unable to walk, dress himself, or even raise his hand to his head. After being stroked by Greatrakes, he had "the perfect use of his arms restored, and could and did rise and walk without pain, help, or difficulty."

Astonishingly, Greatrakes' episode at court ended with these cures. The king's spies had undoubtedly carried out a thorough investigation and concluded that the Irishman was not a threat to the establishment. His close associations with Edward Conway and Robert Boyle were no doubt marks in his favor, as was the fact that his brother-in-law William Godolphin II was England's ambassador to Spain. Even though King Charles II was more tolerant than his father, it is remarkable that Greatrakes was never censored, arrested, or charged with crimes of sedition. While the healer had enemies, no attempt was ever made on his life. The only evidence of King Charles' attitude toward Greatrakes is a passing reference in a letter written by courtier Sir Reginald Graham on April 4, 1666: "The King is far from having a good opinion of his person or his cures."

Some thirty years earlier, another healer, James Leverett, was not as fortunate as Greatrakes. He fell under the scrutiny of the authorities in 1637, during the reign of King Charles I, when a complaint was lodged against him by the king's surgeon. Leverett's investigation dragged on for weeks. His case was not helped by an eleven-year-old girl, who testified in court that Leverett had cured her of the king's evil "when the King couldn't." Like Greatrakes, Leverett rubbed or stroked his patients. Iain and I could not help but wonder if Leverett had ever been to Ireland, where Greatrakes might have seen him. Unlike Greatrakes, Leverett lived in fear for his life. He was beaten up on the road by some "Surgeons or Physitians" and "scarce dares to drink with anyone for fear of poisoning."

Under interrogation by members of the College of Physicians, Leverett testified how healing tired him. The "virtue" goes out of him, he said, "more than when he was a gardener digging up eight roods of ground." He denied that his healing power existed in any article of clothing worn by him, such as gloves or linen, a belief commonly held then. Leverett was found guilty and declared an impostor who "scornfully slighteth his Majesties sacred gift of healing (by his blessed hand) that disease commonly called the King's evil." It is not known what punishment, if any, Leverett received.

While the court no longer bothered Greatrakes, the pressure from other corners in London was unrelenting. Philosopher Joseph Glanvill received a letter from George Rust: "The great discourse now at the coffee-houses, and everywhere is about Mr. G., the famous Irish Stroker . . . some take him to be a conjurer, and some an impostor, but others again adore him as an apostle." An eminent statesman in London assured Greatrakes that he had "made the greatest faction and disturbance between clergy and laymen that anyone has these 1,000 years."

Wonders No Miracles, David Lloyd's attack on Greatrakes, expressed most succinctly and most venomously the objections thrown up by those who feared the religious implications of his cures. Greatrakes was a "miracle monger" and a "cheat." But worse, Lloyd accused him of sedition because he began his healing career by curing the king's evil. If Greatrakes succeeded in diminishing the king's gift of healing and made it appear that the king "could do no more than other men," people would conclude that "he should be no more than other men." Dangerous, indeed.

Greatrakes had heard Lloyd's accusations before, but now in book form, they were broadcast to the world and this hurt him deeply. The healer was so infuriated that he went to the trouble to track down Lloyd. With the eminent physicians Cudworth and Whitchcote at his side, Greatrakes confronted Lloyd and tried to reason with him. Lloyd did not know Greatrakes, had never seen him, so, the healer asked, why the attack? Greatrakes invited Lloyd to his house to witness the cures himself "so that he might be able to relate the truth . . . since he had such an itch to write." Lloyd promised to visit but did not.

Boyle, too, was angered by Lloyd's harangue and insisted that Greatrakes publish a defense to vindicate himself: hence *A Brief Account*. No sooner had he finished the manuscript than Greatrakes fled London, leaving the work with Boyle to carry to completion with the printer.

In the opening of *A Brief Account*, Greatrakes stated outright that his book was an answer to *Wonder No Miracles*, "wherein the author takes . . . to represent me in such black characters, as if I were so horrid a monster, that my very name should affright the reader."

Another point on which Lloyd attacked Greatrakes was the healer's claim that he came to his power after hearing a voice from heaven.

In the seventeenth century, anyone experiencing visions or hearing the voice of God was branded an *enthusiast*, a word derived from the Greek *en-theos*, or "God within." In no uncertain terms, this claim to a direct communication with God was a derogation of church law—a punishable offense. If people began receiving God's truth directly, what need was there of the church? For hundreds of years, the church had developed an elaborate hierarchy with power emanating from the top down. The church's authority was supported by this hierarchy, which dictated that divine knowledge was only accessible through the mediation of the archbishop, bishop, deacon, and so forth. More to the point, without the church's spiritual leverage on the population, how could the institution collect its exorbitant taxes? The church's doctrine dictated that a personal belief about virtually anything was impossible. In effect, free thought was a crime. Maintaining a spiritual monopoly over the population was key to the church's power.

To prove his accusation, Lloyd cited a letter Greatrakes had written to a clergyman in which he purportedly admitted to hearing voices. Greatrakes countered the accusation with a signed affidavit from the same clergyman stating that his letter from Greatrakes contained nothing about voices.

Interestingly, however, while Greatrakes claimed in his book that his talent for curing came to him through three impulses, the explanation he gave to others was often different. In Stubbe's *Miraculous Conformist*, we read that Greatrakes had told him that he "heard frequently a voice within him (audible to none else) encouraging to the trials." Other correspondents as well wrote of Greatrakes' describing his experience in terms of hearing voices.

If Greatrakes chose the word *impulse* to avoid any suggestion that he heard voices, it was likely because of self-imposed censorship; he was fully aware of the dangerous implications of his healings. The state exercised rigorous control over the press, and anyone putting pen to paper for anything—books, tracts, pamphlets, or broadsides—had to obtain royal approval first. Even personal correspondence passing through the postal system was heavily scrutinized. Several months after his sojourn to London, Greatrakes received a letter from a friend in London, warning him of such dangers: "I wish you to be very careful of what you write and to whom ... especially now that letters are so often broke open & exposed to the various scanning & censures of those to whom they were never writ."

But if Greatrakes thought he could protect himself with the word *impulse*, he was wrong. Lloyd was ready to attack. He railed against Greatrakes' "brute impulses." These were "madness . . . the method of Satan" and "contrary to the nature of man." How, one might ask, do people come to these trespasses? By "lying a bed and sleeping . . . by idleness and solitariness . . . by the strength of the passions . . . by windy meats and want of due evacuations." Apparently, Lloyd imagined that Greatrakes suffered from constipation, a sure sign of moral debilitation.

There is an irony here. Were it not for the most scheming and conniving of human machinations, very little, if anything, would be known about Greatrakes. Had David Lloyd not wanted to assassinate

Greatrakes, at least metaphorically, the detractor never would have written *Wonders No Miracles*. Without *Wonders No Miracles*, Greatrakes would never have been moved to write his own book. Were Henry Stubbe not a cunning opportunist, he would not have written *The Miraculous Conformist*. And we must not forget that Boyle, the one person certain to guarantee Greatrakes a measure of immortality, became involved in this story only because of Stubbe's scheming.

Out of this dramatic history there is one amusing document—the ballad "Rub for Rub," billed "A reply in verse, to an attack upon the cures said to be wrought by Valentine Greatrakes." The first time I learned about it in Berkeley, I was intrigued. All we know is that the attack came from a London doctor. That a supporter of Greatrakes would go to the trouble to compose a ballad certain to be heard in the coffeehouses shows the level to which Greatrakes had entered the popular culture. The ballad is made up of eighty-eight stanzas, the best few of which I offer here:

> Come hither, Doctor, and behold in short
> Something of truth, Sir, touching your report.
> You with your beastly stories would delude
> The Faith and Wisdom of the Multitude . . .
> Her Stocking off, he strokes her Lilly-foot,
> What then? The Doctor had made a minde to do't.
> Her Legs, her Knees, her Thighs, a little higher.
> And there's the Doctors Center of Desire . . .

He lays her on the bed, O beastly story!
And then thrusts in his long Suppository,
And tells her on his Faith deny't who can,
Nothing so good for her, as th'Oyl of Man.

Notes and Queries, that simple and thoroughly unpretentious magazine, continued to surprise Iain and me with its enigmatic entries. I was sitting in the British Library, tracking down entries about Greatrakes in the old magazine, when I found the following passage in a letter written in January 1884 by a Mr. J. E. Bailey of Manchester: "I have recently been reading a remarkable set of pamphlets lent me by my good neighbor Samuel Gratix, Esq., of West Point, connected with Valentine Greatraks, who wrought marvelous cures of diseases." It is difficult to read something so startling that you nearly fall out of your chair, but that is what happened to me.

This missive, with phrases such as "a remarkable set of pamphlets" and "my good neighbor Samuel Gratix," could not have been more compelling had the words been uttered by the Oracle of Delphi. The name Greatrakes has many spellings, depending on locale and pronunciation. Greatorix and Gratrix are others. Was this Gratix related to our Greatrakes? What was the "set of pamphlets" he wrote of? How many documents did he have? How could we find his descendants? Were they sitting on these documents and possibly didn't know it?

But the best of *Notes and Queries* came last. In 1953, a Mr. Osborne submitted an entry stating that he was seeking information pertaining to the cache of Greatrakes material mentioned in the 1884 letter. This Osborne was on the same track that Iain and I were on, but with a forty-year head start. He was working on a biography-bibliography of Greatrakes, had obviously seen the 1884 letter, and was trying to track down the same material that we were seeking today. Who was this man Osborne? Did he find the "set of pamphlets"? Had he found other materials on Greatrakes that Iain and I didn't know about? Where could we find a copy of his biography-bibliography? In time, we came to know exactly who this Mr. Osborne was and the surprising circumstances of his work on Greatrakes.

The hunt for a copy of *A Brief Account* had its ups and downs. The downside was that I had not found the book. The upside was that I found other books of great interest from the Greatrakes period. While in Washington, D.C., I stopped into a rare book seller in Georgetown. The chances of finding *A Brief Account* in America were exceedingly slim, but why not? The endorphins people are said to feel after a good physical workout are something I have never experienced. I am quite sure, however, that being surrounded by shelves of worn, leather-bound volumes filled with wonderfully arcane subjects, each beckoning to the mind, can produce a similar effect on the brain. It is quite indescribable.

In this Georgetown bookshop, I came across a small, unassuming book with a most elegant binding. *Rebels No Saints*, published in 1661, was enormously interesting for several reasons. On the inside cover were two bookplates of previous owners. One, the older, was of a Lord Nugent. But the other, smaller and in leather, was of the great American songwriter Jerome Kern.

This book was a verbatim account of the last hours of the regicides before their execution in October 1660—their farewells to loved ones, the words they spoke on their way to the gallows, their final words on the scaffold. Scribes must have been everywhere recording what was said, word for word, as faithfully as if they had microphones in hand.

Thomas Harrison, the first to be executed on October 17, had no doubts about the worth of his cause and even less fear of the outcome. A woman sent to clean his cell and to make a fire for him was asked how he behaved. She answered that "she knew not what he had done, but was sure that he was a good man, and that never such a man was there before, for he was full of God, there was nothing but God in his mouth, so that it would have done anyone good to have been near him. And his discourse and frame of heart would melt the hardest of their hearts."

As the hour of execution approached, Harrison was told to say goodbye to his loved ones. "He parted with his wife and friends with great joy and cheerfulness, as he used to do when going on some journey or about some service for the Lord." When Harrison was told it was time to leave for the gallows at Charing Cross, "he came forth immediately, sooner than was expected, running down the stairs with a smiling countenance."

Harrison was carried to the gallows in a sledge, a large box or wagon without wheels and pulled along the ground by horses amid much pomp. To pour salt on the wound, the gallows had been erected so that Harrison would face the royal palace, Whitehall, "the place where our Sovereign of eternal memory was sacrificed."

Following Harrison was John Cook, a radical lawyer appointed chief prosecutor at the king's trial. Cook had to suffer the gruesome addition of having Harrison's severed head lying next to him in the sledge on his way to the gallows. "Notwithstanding that dismal sight, he passed rejoicingly through the street, as one born up by that spirit which man could not cast down." As he arrived at the execution site and was taken from the sledge, he said, "This is the easiest chariot that ever I rode in my life."

Many of these men had a gift for oratory, and standing on the gallows, they made lengthy and eloquent speeches before being delivered to their fate. Fear and remorse were nowhere in their minds. If anything, the condemned were in an exalted state as they awaited for what they believed would be a literal meeting with their Maker.

Thomas Scot was not allowed to speak for the same amount of time that was given the other regicides on the scaffold. The dramatic exchange between him and the sheriff as Scot was urged to move to his final prayer is well worth reading.

> [Scot began his statement.]"In the beginning of these troubles
> I was unsatisfied. I saw liberties and religion in the nation in great
> danger. I saw the approaches of Popery in great measure, I saw—"

[The sheriff interrupted.]"If you will betake yourself to prayer you may."

[Scot replied.]"I shall not speak to reproach any—"

"You have but little time, Mr. Scot, therefore betake that little time to prayer."

"I shall speak—"

"I beseech you Sir, betake yourself to prayer."

"It may become me to give an account of myself, because—"

"It doth not become you to speak any such thing here, therefore I beseech you to betake yourself to prayer. It is but little time you have to live."

"Tis so—"

"Sir, but when you came upon the Stage you deprived yourself very much."

"I thought to tell you how I came hither—"

"Everybody knows, that—"

"Sirs, tis hard that an Englishman hath not liberty to speak—"

"I cannot suffer you to speak any such thing."

"I shall say no more but this. That it is a very mean and bad cause that will not bear the words of a dying man. It is not ordinarily denied to people in this condition—"

"Sir you had a fair trial and were found guilty."

"Tis according to my mind to speak what may be said—"

"It hath been denied unto your predecessors, and it will be denied unto you."

Scot began to pray. And he went on and on. The hangman, reaching down for a drink of water, told him to hurry it up.

Scot replied, "Pray thee, let me alone. I am not done." He continued his prayer. After going on at length, aggrandizing the Glory of God while deprecating himself, he said something certain to rankle his executioners. "To the praise of God, He hath engaged me in a cause not to be repenteth of." As if this were not enough, he repeated himself, "I say in a cause not to be repented of."

The sheriff interrupted him again. "Is this your prayer Mr. Scot?" Others insisted that he was speaking blasphemy.

Scot continued his prayer. "And thy will be done on earth . . . amen." And he was executed.

Three others followed Scot to the gallows that day. The scene became so gruesome that even the executioner became sick to his stomach and could not continue. His assistant was called upon to carry on in his place. The last execution of the day was Colonel John Jones. He mounted the scaffold "with the like cheerfulness that his brethren did before him." This account can have only a fraction of the impact read here on shiny, new paper compared with the original volume published only a few months after these stirring events.

Several months after my trip to D.C., I was in Los Angeles, and against my better judgment, I stopped in the shop of a rare book dealer. It didn't take long for my book endorphins to kick in. Sitting unpretentiously on a shelf almost out of reach was a book published in 1679, the actual transcript of the trial of the regicides with a customarily long title of the period—*An Exact and Most Impartial Account of the Indictment, Arraignment, Trial and Judgement (according to Law) of Twenty Nine Regicides, The Murtheres of His Late Sacred Majesty of Most Glorious Memory*. Here was the trial, word for word as it happened, with the regicides' defense, as well as the state prosecutor's case against them. A dramatic portion of this document was the sentence read to each man upon his being found guilty. I knew the men's punishment in general terms, but to read the actual sentence as these men heard it, in all its succinctness, is most sobering:

> The judgement of this court is that you be led back to the place from whence you came [jail], and from thence you be drawn upon a hurdle [sledge] to the place of execution, and there you shall be hanged by the neck, and being alive shall be cut down, and your privy parts to be cut off, your entrails to be taken out of your body, and (you living) the same to be burnt before your eyes, and your head to be cut off, your body to be divided into four quarters, and your head and quarters to be disposed of at the pleasure of his King's Majesty, and the Lord have mercy upon your soul.

Sitting with this book put me into quite a state. It wasn't so much because of the stirring reading as it was that I had crossed paths with this book. Finding *Rebels No Saints* was startling enough. But now this? If serendipity, chance, providence, or plain dumb luck was putting these works in my lap, why not *A Brief Account*? The seller assured me he did not have the book, and as I suspected, he had never heard of Valentine Greatrakes. But looking at the shelves of leather volumes surrounding me, I could not help but think, maybe he has it and doesn't know it. I went through the place from end to end.

CHAPTER 5

*L*EAVING LONDON WITHOUT *A Brief Account* left me with an empty feeling. I realized the futility of my search. What if I did find the book? Could I afford it? Worse yet, I was leaving London a few days before a big antiquarian book fair that would gather booksellers from all around Great Britain. At least I had Dublin to look forward to.

I had been to world-class book fairs before. The American Booksellers Association produces such an event every year in California, alternating between San Francisco and Los Angeles. These are truly extraordinary affairs. For the book collector, these fairs are the World Series of book-selling events. Calendars are marked, monies are set aside, and minds are filled with anticipation for days in advance. Several hundred of the finest booksellers from around the world gather in one gigantic hall, where they set up small, elegant booths with the pick of their stock.

Well before the fair begins, hundreds of people line up at the entrance, studying the floor plan in their catalog map and noting the location of the booths of sellers they are interested in. The moment the doors open, an electricity grabs the crowd. The atmosphere becomes what can only be called a controlled state of frenzy. Civility reigns, to be sure, but just underneath the veneer, everyone, at least mentally, is elbowing, jostling, even giving body full blows if need be, to get in first. Heaven help anybody trying to cut in line. I admit, I am no better than anyone else on this count. If I could, I would lock everyone out so that I could peruse at my own pace until I was fully sated.

Once inside, what I really want is a bullhorn. "Attention please! Will the seller who has *A Brief Account,* written by Valentine Greatrakes, London, 1666, please come to the front desk!" Short of this, I walk quickly down the aisles, stopping methodically at each of the British sellers first. If the book does exist and a seller does have it, this is just the type of place where it will be. Two hours later, after it is clear that no one has the book, I begin a second round, scouring the booths of all the other sellers. Confining myself to my particular search is not easy, because there are so many astonishing items of great beauty, many of museum quality. In fact, at the last book fair I attended, I bought one.

A book on Oliver Cromwell is one thing. A book on Cromwell by Samuel R. Gardiner, bound by Zaehnsdorf, is quite another. Published simultaneously in Paris, New York, and Edinburgh in 1899, the book demonstrates the art of bookbinding at its finest, with exquisite crafts-manship in every detail. There were 1,475 copies printed. I bought number 305 of the Paris edition.

While I have had fits of a bibliophilia and have at times slipped into bibliomania (*mania* is the operative part of the word), I am no expert of the book world lingo used to describe the many features of a fine book such as this. The description of this book on Cromwell in that lingo, however, is worth reading, for it has a poetry of its own:

> Gilt top edge, deckled foredge, silk headbands. Full burgundy goat skin binding. Raised bands, gilt spine with decorative tool-ing on both sides of headbands, top and bottom, and in center of panels. Title in gold. Front and back boards: Three decorative bor-der rolls on covers in gold. Floral design motif at corners in gold. Center medallion crest in gold. Silk endpapers and doubleure. Four decorative rolls on doubleure. Single decorative roll to border of endpaper. Double line in gold to board edges. Slight scuffing to corners; otherwise in excellent condition. Illustrated with fine reproductions of Cromwell et al. An exceptionally fine copy.

Ragley! I shoved my notes into my folder and took in the view. The drive across the well-manicured grounds to the main house ended with a groan—Iain's groan. "Oh no, we're too late," he said. We knew that Edward Conway had done extensive remodeling on the mansion after

Ragley Hall

Anne Conway's death, but from the architectural style, Iain could see that little of the original structure was left. We pulled into the parking lot in front of the estate alongside the numerous tour buses and followed the crowds inside. In order to create revenue, the owners of Ragley had turned much of the estate into a museum. Iain was right about these aristocrats not being as rich as they seemed.

The visitor entering the foyer was first greeted by walls covered with greatly enlarged snapshots of the marquis and his wife on their various European trips—a photo of the couple in front of the Fountain of Trevi in Rome, sitting on camels in Egypt, or at the foot of the Eiffel Tower. A large room filled with glass cases displayed the full array of the Crown jewels of England—replicas, that is, all glass. Anything to impress.

We announced ourselves at the main desk and were accompanied into the drawing room, past the crowds of tourists. I quickly glanced around. Fine high ceilings, numerous portrait paintings on the walls, little tables full of elegant knickknacks. The marquis rose from the sofa

Marquis of Hertford in the sitting room of Ragley Hall

to greet us. He was casually dressed in a turtleneck sweater, corduroy jacket (leather patches on the elbows), and baggy corduroy pants. "Please do sit down," he said, leading us to a large sofa. "Would you like some tea? We're terribly routine around here you know, four o'clock and all." Lying on the carpet at the duke's feet was his Great Dane. This was a scene right out of central casting. Tea was served, and we got down to business. The marquis, it turns out, knew little about the estate. He never heard of Greatrakes, and the history we told him about the Conways made little impression on him.

"I did go to the Warwickshire County library once," he said, picking up a sugar cube with silver tongs. "That's where they keep all the archives. I opened this huge drawer and, oh my Lord!" he said, rolling his eyes, "too many pieces of paper, just too many pieces of paper!" "Yes, of course, there are always too many pieces of paper," I assured him. We chatted a bit more, and after tea, he gave us a short tour around the estate, bringing us to a large terrace at the rear of the mansion over-looking geometric gardens dotted with small fountains. The vista was splendid. He pointed to a path leading away from the estate and disappearing up a hillock covered with trees. "In your time, the seventeenth century, that is, they say this was the path leading up to the mansion." Iain and I exchanged a few niceties and thanked the marquis for all his help. I restrained myself from doing a mock curtsy. We left the rear terrace and struck out on the path up the hill to get a view of the land that Greatrakes might have seen in 1666.

From Warwickshire we headed for Derbyshire, to the region where the Greatrakes family originated. The hamlet of Great Rakes no longer existed, but there was proof of the family's origin as we passed the Long Rake mine, still in operation. A quick stop in Wormhill proved that a place with such a name did in fact exist. We visited the small church and walked around the graveyard, searching the tombstones for familiar names but found none.

From there we drove south to Stoke Gabriel, the village where Mary Greatrakes fled with her children at the outbreak of the Irish rebellion in 1641. The village lies in a picturesque setting on the River Dart and was pleasantly nontouristic. Remarkably, the same church where Greatrakes studied still stands, in a setting that has changed little since the seventeenth century. To enter the church, we walked under an ancient, sprawling yew tree, reputedly the oldest tree in England, over one thousand years old. This is the same tree that Valentine walked under as he entered this church. Inside we found a sarcophagus bearing the remains of his teacher, Getseus, and the teacher's wife.

The next morning, we drove on to Stranraer, where we caught the ferry to Larne, on the Irish coast. As we pulled out of the harbor and stood on deck watching the seagulls swoop over the waves in the fog, Iain launched into a short lesson in Anglo-Irish relations.

In 1066, the Normans set out from the west coast of what is now France, invaded England, and succeeded in subjugating the English monarchy. In about 1150, they continued their path of conquest westward over the same waters we were sailing and invaded Ireland, then known as Erin. Rather than killing off the inhabitants and taking their land, the Normans simply pushed out the local rulers, left the peasantry in place with their lands, and told them, "OK, we're in charge now. In the future you'll pay your rents to us." In this way, the Norman overlords amassed great wealth. They left the Gaelic culture intact and, over the centuries, became quite assimilated.

When the Reformation swept across much of Europe in the sixteenth century, Protestantism became the dominant religion in England, and Catholicism was pushed to the margins of English society. Ireland was largely unaffected by the change and remained predominantly Catholic. This epochal shift changed all the relationships between the European nations. The Irish were pushed into closer relations with Catholic Spain. This, in turn, caused the English to fear the Irish because of the certainty, at least to the English, that Spain would use

Ireland as a launching pad to invade England. In this game of international chess, the English, now Protestant, sought to dominate Ireland in order to check Spain's ambitions. Worse yet, England looked on the Catholic Irish as infidels, the anti-Christ—the devil in a habit—worthy only of being crushed.

Through the years, England maintained its desire to occupy Ireland. A few numbers illustrate the drama of this history. In 1603, the English possessed only 10 percent of the land in Ireland. By 1641, this number had reached 41 percent. By 1685, it had risen to 78 percent. Ten years later, the number had increased to 86 percent. The maximum was reached in the 1770s, when England possessed 95 percent of Irish lands.

"And that about sums it up," said Iain, as we watched the shores of Larne appear out of the fog. Once in Ireland, we drove to Belfast, to the library at Queens University. Our only find was an article in an Irish journal, a piece of sheer fantasy written by a local history buff. The writer tells the preposterous story of Greatrakes living in "an historic castle at Affane" and being summoned to London to cure King Charles II, who was "seriously ill and facing death from an incurable disease." The king made a complete recovery and offered Greatrakes a beautiful home in London and "a substantial annuity for the rest of his life." More absurd, on his death, Greatrakes' body was transported to Affane for burial. He made this final voyage "across the Irish Sea by schooner and with its Royal emblems flying at half-mast."

Iain's list of contacts in the world of academia is enviable. During our travels, we met noted scholars such as Roy Porter, James Jacobs, and Michael Hunter. We met the venerable Christopher Hill, the doyen of seventeenth-century English history, at his home in Sibford Ferris. While they all knew of Greatrakes, he was far too minor a player on the world stage to have taken up much of their time. Clearly, Iain and I were fast attaining the distinction of becoming the world's experts on Valentine Greatrakes.

While in Belfast, we dined at the home of a friend of Iain's. Fiona was a true Irish beauty with long, red hair, lovely green eyes, high cheekbones, and alabaster skin. After dessert, we sat talking in candlelight, sipping wine, and on a whim, I suggested that each of us sing a song. Iain sang an English ballad, I sang one of the few folk songs I knew, and Fiona, believe it or not, sang—what else?—"Danny Boy." Sitting across from her as she sang, I felt the same inadequacy as when I stood before the Grand Canyon and realized that my senses were far too meager to take in the full scope of the beauty before me.

From Belfast we traveled on to Dublin and the National Library of Ireland. We checked into a B and B and went directly to the library. Like the British Library although much smaller, this reading room is circular and capped with an elegant dome. Whereas the British Library has an old-world elegance in the grand style, the smaller National Library of Ireland rings of a homey quaintness. To obtain our reader's cards, we were led into the office of Elizabeth Kirwan for an interview. Her stern expression told us that she had been doing this for a long time. But the name Valentine Greatrakes broke the ice. "Oh, every now and then we do get someone in here looking for him," she said smiling. "For the most part he's forgotten, but in his own time he caused quite a stir, I'm told." We chatted for a few minutes about the history of the period as she completed the paperwork. Cards in hand, Iain and I divided up the work and agreed to meet at noon.

Noon came, and we sat down to compare notes. Iain looked as if he had just seen a ghost. "What's the matter?" I asked. "You won't believe it," he said, sliding a book in front of me—*Irish Witchcraft and Demonology.* I was stupefied. Greatrakes, an amateur witch finder!

The witch-hunt craze that terrorized Europe for almost three hundred years had little effect in Ireland. Whereas countries like Germany, France, and Switzerland were paralyzed with fear as inquisitors condemned thousands to the stake, during the entire duration of this holocaust, barely a half dozen trials for witchcraft were recorded in all of Ireland. One of the most famous of these trials was that of Florence Newton, in Youghal in September 1661. It was at this trial that Greatrakes appeared.

Newton, an itinerant beggar in Youghal, knocked at the door of John Pyne's house one day, begging for food. Pyne's servant girl, Mary Longdon, answered and turned Newton away empty-handed. Angered by the rebuff, Newton went off, swearing. About a week later, the two women met on the road. Newton, feeling remorseful for her outburst, "violently kissed" Longdon, exclaiming, "I pray thee, let thee and I be friends, for I bear thee no ill will, and I pray thee, do thou bear me none." About a month later, the servant girl fell ill with hallucinations and violent fits in which she would "vomit up needles, pins, horsenails, stubbs, wool, and straw."

Longdon accused Newton of bewitching her and pressed charges. The English court practiced a number of methods to determine whether a woman was a witch. In one method, known as the water experiment, or swimming the witch, the suspect was tied up, toes to her thumbs, and thrown into a lake or pond. If the woman sank, she was innocent. If she floated, she was guilty. The logic was simple. Any woman, on becoming a witch, was obligated to enter into a pact with the devil, vowing to reject everything to do with the church, including the baptismal water. If the woman floated in the water, it was a sign that the baptismal water was refusing her, because she had refused it, which was proof of guilt. If she sank, this meant the baptismal water was accepting her because she had accepted it, and hence, was a sign of innocence.

The mayor of Youghal contemplated carrying out this ordeal but decided against it. Greatrakes was present at the trial with two friends and told the judge that they had read of a method to determine whether a woman was a witch. The judge asked them to proceed. The three men sat Newton on a stool and asked a shoemaker present at the inquiry to try to pierce the stool with his awl. He tried twice and failed. The third time, he succeeded. The shoemaker pulled the awl out of the stool and found that the tip of the blade had snapped off. The men searched for the blade tip but could not find it, or any mark of a blade in the stool. This was probably taken as proof of Newton's supernatural powers.

One of the men then placed the awl in Longdon's hand and ran toward Newton's hand, trying to pierce it but could not. The awl blade was so bent by the force of the thrust that it could not be straightened again. One man, Mr. Blackwall, next took a lance and cut into Newton's hand. She did not bleed. This too must have been taken as a sign of her power. Blackwall cut the other hand, which did bleed. No more is known of the trial. There is no record of the verdict, although according to historian Samuel Hayman, Florence Newton was executed.

Just then a voice came over the library speaker, "Closing in five minutes. Please return your materials," and so forth. Iain and I packed up and walked over to Bewley's Café on Grafton Street. In 1661, Greatrakes is party to sticking women with knives; the following year, he begins healing. Where's the sense?

That Greatrakes would go from witch finder to healer within the space of a year seems like a startling conversion. In a larger sense, Iain pointed out, a "conversion" was not really necessary, since witch finding and magical healing were two complementary sides—the diabolical and the divine—of Christian theology.

"What did you come up with?" Iain asked. My find was less gruesome but just as interesting—a small notebook of letters written to Greatrakes in the 1660s by a friend in England, Sir Edmundbury Godfrey. The number of well-known names surrounding Greatrakes was impressive. Some I recognized: Robert Boyle, William Penn, Joseph Glanvill, and, later, Samuel Mather (grandfather of Cotton Mather, of the infamous Salem witch trials of the 1690s). But Sir Edmundbury Godfrey I did not. Godfrey, I learned, was the most popular magistrate in Britain. He presided over the 1678 trial of Titus Oates, ringleader of the infamous Popish Plot, a scheme to assassinate King Charles II and reestablish Catholicism in England. Sometime after this trial, Godfrey was brutally murdered under mysterious circumstances.

In a letter dated 1667, Godfrey referred to Greatrakes' life in Affane and confirmed the healer's pleasure of living in the country: "I am mightily pleased with your heavenly expressions of the contentment which you find and enjoy in your retired, innocent and virtuously industrious country life which ingenious description of yours, put me in mind of paradise."

We also read of Greatrakes' relationship with his wife, Ruth. In a previous letter, Greatrakes had apparently spoken of his wife in the most glowing terms. Godfrey responded, "But that you should find and enjoy such a woman, and a wife, and a mother of children, is a miracle of miracles, next to that of the Virgin Mary."

Godfrey's writings reflected Christian attitudes toward women as inferior beings. Ruth's perfection, he thought, "seems to represent a new creation," for "the original stock of grace and virtue is long since decayed and lost in that sex." He advised that to keep Ruth in her "country innocence," Greatrakes should not let "the discourses of London and Whitehall enter into her ears, or affect her fancy."

The next day at the National Library of Ireland, while waiting for an item to be delivered to my reading table, I browsed the catalogs on the shelves, looking through the Gs. There I found a listing for an item about Greatrakes I had not seen before. I filled out a request slip, and a few minutes later, a gentleman walked up and placed a cardboard folder on the table in front of me. Inside was an original letter written by Greatrakes in 1649. Historic documents such as these are usually bound into large binders along with other documents. This letter was loose in its folder. It had all the freshness of a letter that had just arrived with the morning mail. Greatrakes was twenty-one years old and was writing to the Duke of Ormonde. The young man was trying to regain his family's lands, which had been confiscated by the native Irish during the rebellion of 1641 or, as he put it, that were in the possession of his father "before [these] unhappy distractions." I had read of this quotation months earlier, but here was the original document.

During our short stay in Dublin, I managed to get away long enough to find the rare book sellers. The name Greatrakes always elicited the same blank stares. More exhilarating were the humbler used book stores. Here my fantasies ran wild. The shelves marked "History" were full of dusty, old tomes, enough to get me salivating. I admit that under the calm demeanor of a middle-aged man gently perusing books, there lies a madman on a quest. By now my mind was so honed to this search that my fingers seemed to know where to go before my eyes could see anything. Slender, leather-bound volumes with titles so worn that they could not be read were prime candidates for a possible stupendous find.

The most inconspicuous books lying on top of rows of other books, or pushed to the back of the shelf between two larger books, did not escape me. I had to see everything.

While working on Greatrakes, I began a project concerning Paris history that eventually became a guide to Paris. Along with the name of Greatrakes etched inside my nostrils, I was also on the lookout for good books on Paris history. One day, I was in a used-book-store in Berkeley and had a feeling. The shelves of history books were full of uninteresting items, but something in my head made me keep looking. I went through every book. The highest shelf of books extended into a storage space past a wall divider that I had not noticed. I passed through a door I was not supposed to go through and got onto a ladder that happened to be there. Fortunately, the shopkeeper was not in sight. The last books on the shelf were just out of reach and needed a good stretch on my part. But it was the very last of the last books on this shelf that proved to be the find. A Baedeker's guide to Paris, 1867, in mint condition with all the maps. I nearly fell off the ladder. This only fueled my search for *A Brief Account*.

Iain and I left Dublin and headed south for Cashel, where we planned to spend the night. Approaching town from the north, we came upon one of the most spectacular archeological sites in Ireland—the Rock of Cashel. Situated high on a limestone mound, the Rock was chosen by the Eoghanachta clan from Wales in the fourth century as the base of their power in the region. The site passed into the hands of the church in the twelfth century. Today one sees striking remains, including the fortification surrounding the Rock, an impressive thirteenth-century cathedral, a tower dating from the eleventh or twelfth century, and a twelfth-century chapel.

We checked into Finerty's Bed & Breakfast and, after a walk around town, settled in for an early dinner at the hotel. Afterward, we struck up a conversation with the owner, Brian, and his friend Tony. Brian was fit looking, with the ruddy complexion of someone who had spent years outdoors. His corpulent friend puffed away on his pipe, with his chin hidden behind the collar of his oversized turtleneck sweater. We mentioned the name Greatrakes and got no reaction. But when we said the word "healer," they both lit up like lightbulbs. "Oh, that stuff's been goin' on here for years," said Brian, "and don't think it's a thing of the past, either! Not by a long shot it ain't."

Tony leaned forward over his beer mug. "You're darn right," he said. "Why, about two years ago, I had a terrible case of sciatica, the worst pain I ever endured. So I went to see Jimmy the Bonesetter." I chuckled to myself. Jimmy the Bonesetter—sounds like a Mafia hit man. "There I was, sitting on the chair," he said. "He takes one look at me, puts his hands right here," Tony placed his hands on his midsection, "and one-two-three, crack! Never had any pain since then."

Brian nodded his head in agreement. "Now me, I had a slipped disc. Was about three or four years ago. It hurt so bad they had to carry me in. Jimmy saw me lyin' on the couch, took hold of me, did a little this and that, and I walked out feelin' fine. Never had a bit of pain or discomfort again."

Iain and I sat silent, uncomprehending. "You think that's something?" Brian said. "Listen to this. Some years ago, there was this farmer nearby who owned a racehorse worth millions! But the poor creature had ringworm. They couldn't sell the animal for love or money. The best vets came from Europe and America, but no one could do a thing. Next thing you know, someone brings this old woman by from the neighborhood. They said she had a way with animals. She had a jar of something that looked like lard and rubbed it on the horse's forehead. A couple of day's later, the ringworm was gone. Gone! Woman's gone, too. Too bad," he said, shaking his head.

Iain and I looked at each other. Nothing had changed in three hundred years. "Oh, it's been goin' on for a long time," Brian said. "It's from the folkways, handed down from person to person. Tradition, you know." Of course, we wanted to meet Jimmy, and Brian phoned him, but he refused to see us. He was too afraid of publicity. I tried to explain our work, that we were not about publicity. I mentioned Greatrakes but to no avail. He would not see us.

Before going to Affane, we decided to head first to Lismore, to visit the Waterford County Library. On our way, we passed through the winding roads of the Knockmealdown Mountains. I did not know of these mountains and had not expected them. We were motoring through pleasant, hilly countryside until we drove around a bend, and in one fell swoop, a vista hit my eyes as nothing had ever done before. Stretching as far as the eye could see was one vast, rolling patchwork of farmland made up of different shades of deep, rich green, all sectioned off by low stone walls and overgrown hedges. The bright sun and blue skies brought out the full richness of the countryside and made it clear where the name *Emerald Isle* comes from.

The landscape one sees today in Ireland is vastly different from the Ireland of the seventeenth century. Then, the whole province of Munster had been intentionally deforested by the English. One reason was to deny the Irish rebels any hiding places. Another was the great traffic in timber export that helped fill the queen's coffers. Also, many of the English settlers maintained large ironworks and other types of industry that required wood for fuel. The greatest concentration of trees was on the estates owned by the English. There one typically found elms, walnuts, sycamores, and spruces.

Driving to Lismore, Iain and I passed a large billboard on the road exclaiming in large letters, GERMAN HEALER. "Good Lord, can you believe it!" he said. We screeched into a U-turn and pulled into a gravel drive leading up to a house trailer parked behind a main house. A sign on the metal door indicated that the healer was in. We knocked and were greeted by the healer's Irish wife, a tall, buxom brunette dressed in a white lab coat. "My husband's busy right now," she said. "But if you don't mind waiting in my office for a few minutes, he'll be right with you." I was having a bad bout of chronic heartburn, I told her, and maybe he could help.

She led us down a narrow corridor, whose walls were punctuated with an array of news articles on successful cures, and into an overheated, tiny office barely large enough for three chairs and a small desk. Then, the most bizarre scene ensued. Seated in this cramped space, she proceeded to tell us about her passion for writing murder mysteries and added casually, "Oh well, we have a few minutes, so why don't I just read you a couple of pages?" She then launched into reading us a gruesome story of murder and mayhem. A young man, spurned by his lover and desperately jealous, decides the only just solution is murder. Unfortunately, he mistakenly kills the girl's identical twin sister. The description of the murder was not lacking in detail: flashing knives, blood, the lust for revenge. She read on and on, at various points showing us colorful collages she had made using photos cut out of magazines to illustrate the high points of her story. To complete this bizarre scene, hanging on the wall behind her was a large, framed picture of Jesus looking down on us. I shot a sideways glance at Iain. He fought to keep his eyes open. The long drive, stifling heat, and boring reading were taking their toll. Then she slapped her folder shut. "Well now, boys, what did you think? Did you like it? I've had a few people over from town to hear it, and they were quite please-d." Iain and I mumbled something about how evocative it was, gripping, and so on. She reached into the filing cabinet next to her. "I've got another short one here. I'll just read you a bit if you don't mind." Suddenly, the door flung open, and her husband stuck his head in. Saved by the healer! Unfortunately, this was the most good he did for me that day. As we left, I glanced down the corridor and saw a waiting room full of patients.

As we arrived in Lismore, our adrenaline kicked into high gear. Only four miles from Affane—this was definitely Greatrakes country. We checked into the main hotel in town and walked across the street to the Waterford County Library. The library's collection was housed in two small rooms and contained enough material to keep us busy for days. Unfortunately, we only had hours. Methodically I went over the shelves, pulling off anything that seemed remotely connected to Greatrakes while Iain thumbed through the indexes—the Gs, that is—and stacked up books with pages that we needed to photocopy. Land survey maps from the nineteenth century showed the exact location of Affane and the Greatrakes house on the east bank of the Blackwater River. The maps also showed the original house, which was built on the west bank by his grandfather in the 1580s and was known as Norrisland. Did anything remain?

Librarian Evelyn Coady, excited that two men from California were so involved in this local history (she knew of Greatrakes), raced back and forth to help us at the copy machine in the next room. Even though she ran the place, closing time was closing time. At the stroke of five, the door locked behind us and we headed across the street to the pub to examine our new material.

In any historical study, if one can go beyond the mere facts to penetrate to the humanity of the subject, to the feelings of the people involved, and if one can empathize with those people in any respect, then time is no longer a barrier and what may chronologically be hundreds of years ago is right there before you. An example is the Battle

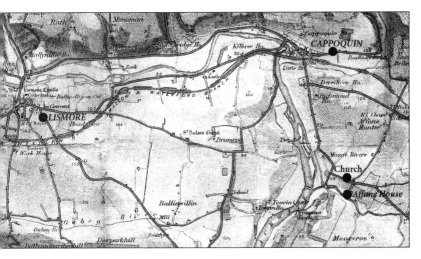

Map showing Lismore to the left, Cappoquin at top right, and
Affane House and Church in the bottom right-hand corner

of Affane, fought on the Greatrakes land in 1565, some twenty years before the first Greatrakes arrived in Ireland. This is a remarkable story worth retelling.

For hundreds of years, the two dominant families in this region of Munster were Old English: the Desmonds and the Ormonds. The two clans feuded incessantly over land. In 1532, they were brought together when, à la *West Side Story*, Joan Desmond married into the Ormond family. Everyone rejoiced. The union of the two adversaries was seen by all as a blessed event bringing to an end the clan wars. As part of her dowry, Joan brought to the Ormonds a number of disputed lands that the two families had been warring over for centuries.

When Joan's husband died sixteen years later, she married another Ormond, but a few years later, he died too, in a battle at Clonmel. In 1553 she married again, but this time back into her own clan. Now that she was back in the Desmond fold, her kin demanded the return of the lands she had brought to the Ormonds as part of her first marriage's dowry. The Ormonds refused to give up the lands. The peace between the two clans was again on shaky ground. In 1560, after seven years of a heated standoff, the two clans made preparations for what was to be the decisive battle. The rival armies met about one mile from Tipperary, the Desmonds with an army almost five thousand strong, and the Ormonds close in number, with the addition of some cannon.

Joan arrived in a panic before the two sides could join in battle. On one side were the Desmonds, led by her husband, Gerald. On the other side stood the Ormonds, led by her now-grown son, Maurice. For fourteen days, the grief-stricken woman ran back and forth from one camp to the other, imploring the two men she loved most, her husband and her son, to settle the dispute peacefully. Amazingly, she prevailed and the rival armies dispersed.

For five years, there was a fitful peace marked by skirmishes from both sides while councils and commissions tried to resolve the dispute. In January 1565, Joan Desmond died. Less than one month later, the inevitable clash took place. The Desmonds were on their way to carry out a surprise punitive action against the Ormond castle at Dromana, just south of Affane. Instead the tables turned, and it was they who were ambushed by the Ormonds at the Affane crossroads. The fighting did not last long, and the victory went to the Ormonds. There were about three hundred fatalities, with many slaughtered or drowned in the Blackwater and Finisk rivers.

The Desmonds recovered from this defeat and eventually prospered again. But war was a way of life for the clans, and when they weren't fighting each other, they always had the English to go after. In 1579, the Earl of Desmond led one of the many insurrections attempting to oust the English from Ireland. The poet Edmund Spenser described horrific scenes of this bloody conflict: "Out of every corner of the woods and glens, [people] came creeping forth upon their hands, for their legs could not bear them. They looked like anatomies of death; they spoke like ghosts crying out of their graves."

Spenser, "the gentle poet" of *The Faerie Queene*, was among the most vicious in his position toward Ireland. He advocated a scorched-earth policy to subjugate the Irish and starvation for those who resisted English domination: "Great must be the instrument, but famine must be the meane, for till Ireland can be famished, it cannot be subdued." In 1582, more than thirty thousand men, women, and children were starved to death in Munster.

During the course of the rebellion, the English confiscated the Desmond land, section by section. By the end of the rebellion, they had confiscated some three hundred thousand acres of land. The goal of the English was to take the land and to people it with English. A few years earlier, the English Lord Justice Pelham, anticipating an Ireland empty of Irish, imagined a land that would become like "well tempered wax, apt to take such form and point as her Majesty will put upon it."

Toward this goal, the English divided the confiscated Desmond land into large plots, called *seignories*, of twelve thousand acres each. Each seignory was then assigned to a wealthy Englishman who agreed to populate the land with English soldier-farmers and artisans, and to carry on an industry profitable to the Crown. In principle, these English families were not allowed to employ any "mere Irish," that is, native Irish.

One of the most notable of the English to obtain a seignory was Sir Walter Raleigh, who became the largest landowner in the region, with a vast estate of forty-two thousand acres, part of which included the Greatrakes lands at Affane. Among the various endeavors he undertook on the land, Raleigh planted large fruit orchards, including the first cherry trees in Ireland, which he imported from the Canary Islands.

The Crown's dream of an Ireland without any Irish, however, was never realized. The proprietors were absentee landlords who never succeeded in recruiting enough English to resettle in frontier conditions surrounded by a hostile native population. In the end, the colonists had no choice but to allow large numbers of Irish onto their land.

In time, Raleigh tired of his obligations and sold off his lands in Ireland. And this brings us back to Robert Boyle. It was his father,

Richard, the Great Earl, who bought the lands from Raleigh. This is why Robert Boyle was born in Ireland, at Lismore Castle, a mere one hundred yards from where Iain and I were sitting. The castle was built in the 1590s by Sir Walter Raleigh and came into the hands of Richard Boyle as part of the lands he bought from Raleigh. The castle's crenellated towers, its prominent position on the river, and its lush, woodsy setting make it the picture of sixteenth-century Ireland. In 1753, the castle came into the hands of the Duke of Devonshire and has remained with that family to this day.

It is one of the great ironies of this story that Robert Boyle and Valentine Greatrakes, born two years apart and only four miles from each other, never met as children, because of the vast difference in their social classes, and then years later became so embroiled in London. The Greatrakes family was wealthy by any standard of the day, but Robert Boyle's father Richard, the 1st Earl of Cork (known as the "Great Earl"), was the wealthiest man in the entire kingdom. The elder Boyle achieved his wealth the old-fashioned way: through bribery, fraud, and corruption. In his ascent up the economic ladder, he became a notorious swindler and plunderer whose sole aim in life was to increase his wealth at the expense of anyone who crossed his path.

Richard Boyle arrived in Ireland in 1588, the year of the Armada, with little more than the clothes on his back. He obtained the position of deputy escheator for Queen Elizabeth, a job that consisted of traveling through the region of Munster to verify the land titles of the local Irish gentry. Farmers with titles out of order had their lands

Richard Boyle, Great Earl of Cork, father of Robert Boyle

confiscated in the name of the Crown. For families that had been on the land for hundreds of years, what chance was there that they would have a title? All the better for the Crown. In return for his services, Boyle received a percentage of the confiscated lands and thus began amassing his great fortune. When Sir Walter Raleigh tired of managing his lands at Affane, he sold them to Boyle.

The contrast between father and son Boyle could not be greater. While the father thought only of his own gain, Robert led a reclusive life as a pious Christian, devoted to the study of science and religion. All of his endeavors were aimed toward the production of "fruits" that could benefit all people. While the father made powerful enemies who sought to destroy him, the son was highly respected and recognized as a "Christian gentleman" who lived his life in accordance with the high morality of his deep religious beliefs. Richard's religion went as far as the belief that his success in life had been preordained, that Divine Providence had guided him in his journey toward wealth. He married twice and had fifteen children. Robert never married and remained celibate his entire life.

More than Richard Boyle's unscrupulous rise to power, it is his second marriage, to Catherine Fenton, that boggles the modern mind. The story I came across in my research is so implausible yet so good that I want to recount it here. Boyle met his future wife Catherine Fenton when she was only two years old. This was on a visit with her father, Sir Jeoffrey Fenton, the English secretary of state for Ireland. Boyle saw a good match in the infant and asked Fenton if he would accept him for his son-in-law. Fenton asked Boyle if he "would stay for her." Boyle agreed and Fenton gave his consent. Apparently, Boyle did not stay all that well, for in 1595, he married Joan Apsley, a woman of means. She died four years later in childbirth. In 1603, Boyle fulfilled his old agreement and married Catherine Fenton, then around seventeen years old. The couple made their home at Lismore Castle.

Catherine produced children at breakneck speed, fifteen within the space of twenty-one years, and as was customary among the nobility, she took no part in the first five years of their upbringing, as they were all put out to a wet nurse. Catherine and Richard's seventh son and fourteenth child, born in 1627, was Robert. Catherine Fenton died of consumption two years later, at age forty-one.

The same year that he married Catherine, Richard Boyle was knighted by Queen Elizabeth. In 1620, he reached the height of his social climbing and was anointed the Great Earl of Cork. Thirteen years later, he was appointed Lord High Treasurer of the kingdom. His downfall began over a bitter land dispute with the Crown—a dispute that left him £15,000 poorer and very ill. The coup de grâce came with the outbreak of the Great Rebellion of 1641. The Irish rebels reclaimed his vast landholdings, and no land meant no rents. In a short time his fortune was depleted. He died in 1643, a broken man.

My search for a copy of *A Brief Account* continued. Often, I'd tell myself, "Give it up. You'd just as well win the lottery." But no sooner was I in the vicinity of a rare book store than my senses sharpened and I went into hunting mode. The fact that I was finding other seventeenth-century books relevant to the Greatrakes period heightened my anticipation of finding *the* book.

In 1994, while visiting family in Detroit, I learned of a rare book seller on the outskirts of Ann Arbor. Behind a house full of books was a large barn full of even more books. Most were twentieth century, but at the sight of a long row of shelves jammed with eighteenth- and nineteenth-century bindings, my nostrils flared. There was no Greatrakes, but I did find something intensely interesting: *The Wars in England, Scotland & Ireland Containing an Account of all the Battles, etc.*, by Robert Burton, 1737. This book, so small that it could fit into a shirt pocket, was so packed with vivid history that one would expect the pages to be writhing and bouncing on the shelf. Along with an account of numerous wars, this book contained a most compelling transcript of the trial of King Charles I by the Cromwellians in 1648. Incredibly, the book recorded his last words and actions on the scaffold as he was about to be beheaded. If, as the saying goes, life is in the details, then the details of this reading are enough to make one's hair stand on end with the immediacy of it all.

On the first day of the king's trial at Westminster Hall, a long list of charges was read to him, accusing him of being a tyrant, traitor, and murderer. The king was asked to enter a plea of guilty or not guilty. He refused. He would not recognize the authority of the court and thus refused to enter a plea. For the next three days, the king and the court parried, the court trying every maneuver, every line of reasoning, to force a plea, with the king deftly deflecting each move, trying the patience of the court, pushing it from frustration to frustration. Finally, with no choice left, the court found the king guilty by default.

During the proceedings, Burton wrote, "Two things were remarkable." First, as the king sat on his crimson velvet chair facing his accusers, the silver head of his staff accidentally fell off. He did not move, but waited for someone to pick it up. No one approached, so he bent down, picked it up himself, and put it in his pocket. Second, as the king was escorted from the hall on the first day of the proceedings, he looked at the court "with an austere countenance," and pointing his staff at a sword lying nearby, said, "I do not fear that." Leaving the hall, some people cried out, "God save the King." Others cried for justice. On Saturday, January 27, 1649, the sentence was read—decapitation.

On the morning of January 30, 1649, with drums beating and flags flying, the king, accompanied by a regiment of soldiers, left Saint James and walked to Whitehall. At his side were his two close friends, Doctor

Juxon and Colonel Tomlinson. After receiving the last sacrament, he drank a glass of claret and ate a bit of bread and then waited. His children were brought in for farewells. (His young daughter, Elizabeth, died of grief several months later at Carisbrooke Castle.) At 1 PM he walked to the scaffold, which was draped in black for the occasion. Mounted horsemen kept the enormous crowd far enough back so that the throng could not hear his final words.

On the scaffold, the king saw the block and asked if it could be set a little higher. Then he spoke, proclaiming his innocence, justifying his actions, and declaring himself a good Christian. Twice during his lengthy final statement, he warned several men standing nearby on the scaffold not to touch the blade of the executioner's axe, for fear that they would dull it. "Hurt not the axe that it may hurt me." The king then gave instructions to the executioner—he would pose his head on the block, recite a short prayer, and, when done, thrust his hands out to signal the axe to fall. He then asked Juxon for a nightcap to hold his long hair.

This done, the king turned to the executioner and asked, "Does my hair trouble you?" and was asked to put it more fully under the cap, which he did with the help of the executioner and the bishop. When everything was in place, Juxon said to the king, "There is but one stage more, this stage is turbulent and troublesome, it is a short one." The king replied, "I go from a corruptible to an uncorruptible crown." Juxon, affirming this, said, "You are exchanged from a temporal to an eternal crown. Good exchange." Once more, the king asked the executioner, "Is my hair well?" Satisfied that he was ready, the king took off his cloak and several vests until he was down to his waistcoat, and then put the cloak back on. Then, looking at the block, he said to the executioner, "You must set it fast." He wanted to make sure the block would not move. "It is fast Sir," was the reply. "When I put my hands out this way, stretching them out, then—" The king stood for a moment, his hands and eyes toward the sky, and he said two or three words. He then knelt down and laid his head on the block, but his hair fell out of the cap. As the executioner bent down to arrange it under the cap again, the king thought he was going to strike and said, "Wait for the sign!" "I will and it please your majesty," said the executioner. The king said a short prayer, stretched out his hands, and the executioner severed his head from his body with one blow.

CHAPTER 6

ONE DAY, MY PURSUIT of the Gs led me to something extremely interesting, which I found in the most unusual of places. I was visiting an aunt in her posh suburban ranch house outside Detroit and noticed bookshelves lined with what are known as "books by the yard." These are Victorian-era leather-bound books bought by interior decorators for clients as a kind of theatrical decor. The books are not meant to be read, but are meant only to be seen. They are bought by the yard to fill a given length of shelf space. Titles, therefore, are unimportant, as is language. On my aunt's shelf, I noticed ten fine, leather-bound volumes of the *Dictionnaire Historique*, published in Paris in 1810. I opened up to the Gs, and there I found "Greaterick (Valentine)." Ah, the incongruity of it all. The text, in French, was most interesting and most unflattering.

The Irish imposter came from a good house and made a great noise in 1665/66. He was man of great simplicity in his manner who believed he could cure the king's evil. He touched a number of people who he pretended to heal. Three years later he believed, or wanted to believe, that he could cure an epidemic fever that was killing many people in Ireland. He was followed thereafter by a multitude of people. As his reputation grew he boasted that his power to cure grew also. In his folly he went so far as to think there were no diseases he could not cure. This charlatan attributed all sickness to spirits and demoniacal possession. The King summoned him to Whitehall where the court was not very persuaded of his gift for miracles. Not having succeeded at court, this deranged man went to the city where he was highly sought after. He was always surrounded by an incredible number of people in all conditions of sickness seeking his touch. He did not, however, persuade the philosophers. He was verbally attacked, but he did have his defenders, even among the doctors. He published a letter addressed to the celebrated Boyle along with a number of certificates signed by theologians attesting to the authenticity of his cures. Despite these attestations his reputation did not hold up long in England. His cures were due, not so much to pretended miracles, as they were to the gullibility of the public. It was noted that he touched women more attentively than men and was obliged to disappear. [*translation mine*]

The source the *Dictionnaire Historique* cited for this material was a work entitled *The Irish Prophet,* written in 1666 by another figure renowned in his own time yet forgotten today, the French writer Charles de Saint-Evremond. Writer, soldier, and wit, Saint-Evremond fell into disgrace after voicing dissent against the treaty of 1659 known as the Peace of the Pyrenees, and he was driven into exile. He lived in England for forty years and is the only Frenchman to be buried in Westminster Abbey.

Although I was surprised to see Greatrakes' reputation extend as far as 1810, I was even more surprised to see Greatrakes crop up again in the 1860s. The healer's name popped up in the most unlikely of places, in *The Humbugs of the World,* by the great master of humbuggery himself, P. T. Barnum: "As for the quacks, patent medicines and universal remedies, I need only mention their names. Prince Hohenlohe, Valentine Greatrakes, John St. John Long, Doctor Graham and his wonderful bed, Mesmer and his tub, Perkins' metallic tractors—these are half a dozen. Modern history knows hundreds of such." And later, in 1877, Madame Blavatsky, founder of the theosophical movement, wrote in *Isis Unveiled* about "real and God-like healers" and refers to the "well-known" Valentine Greatrakes as "the ignorant and poor Irishman."

But one night, in around 1995, a more intentional kind of browsing bore even more interesting fruit. I was in a Berkeley bookstore and came upon a most exciting title, *The World of the Muggletonians.* I recognized the name Muggletonian, a radical religious sect that arose during the English civil war, but I knew little more. I pulled the volume off the shelf, paged to the index, and headed for the Gs. There I found Valentine Greatrakes! I could not get to page 48 fast enough. I gazed at the few lines about him and sank onto a bench beside me. Within moments, Iain's and my careful picture of Greatrakes came apart at the seams. This man who had carefully fashioned himself into a devout Anglican obedient to the Church of England was apparently far more radical in his religious views than we had surmised. Greatrakes was probably not a Muggletonian in the strict sense of the word, but was clearly sympathetic to both the sect and its founder, Ludovic Muggleton. Most enigmatic was the mention that Greatrakes had penned "some very Muggletonian sounding verse." In the book's endnotes, a reference for this verse was given to papers in the British Library. Why hadn't Iain and I come across this before? The following year, we found this document in the Manuscript Room of the British Library. Because the document had not been cross-indexed, it was cataloged under "Muggleton."

Iain was surprised by this association too and gave me some background. As the English state crumbled during the civil war, the old religious prohibitions crumbled as well. Cromwell's New Model Army of insurgents was rampant with freethinkers who sprouted a whole variety of radical religious sects: Quakers, Levellers, Ranters, Anabaptists, Fifth Monarchists, and Muggletonians. The Quakers are the only sect from that period to survive today. All these sects were founded on a belief that the established church was corrupt and in need of reform. Sacred features of the church, like marriage vows, a structured clergy, and the immortality of the soul, were tenets held in dispute.

The Muggletonians were never great in number, nor did they ever pose a real threat to the established church. Nevertheless, any nonconformist group was deemed intolerable by the state and had to be quashed. The sect rejected much of the church's dogma, including the institution of priesthood and baptism, as well as the physical structure of the church itself (the members of the sect preferred to meet in pubs). Muggletonians also rejected the orthodox belief in a devil that "dwells within the bodies of men and women" and instead viewed the devil as an autonomous, corporeal being that results from "man's spirit of unclean reason and carnal imagination." Placing the devil outside the individual rather than within propagates a belief in the worth of individual conscience—a heretical thought in itself—and gives people a degree of responsibility that the Church of England would never accept. Personal responsibility carries with it the right to think for oneself and to make choices. People might even go so far as to decide for themselves what is right and wrong.

This discovery sent Iain and me straight back to Greatrakes' friend Robert Phaire, the regicide, but this time for a closer reading. During one of Greatrakes' trips to England, he hand-delivered letters from Phaire to Ludovic Muggleton. This seemingly innocent act was now thick with meaning and should have been a clue the first time we encountered it. Within the tensions of the period, association was everything. Phaire would never have asked Greatrakes to deliver goods to someone who would have been an insult to Greatrakes' own religious beliefs. With this new revelation, more pieces of the puzzle fell into place. Phaire had been a member of the Ranters and Quakers during the late 1640s and the 1650s and had become a Muggletonian around 1662. We had not given this much thought, however. Nor had it occurred to us that Greatrakes might have been influenced by the milieu of radicalism that surrounded him during the seven years he spent in Cromwell's army.

This split between the public and private Greatrakes cast everything into a new light. What were his real thoughts and feelings? What words did he speak in private but never dare utter in public? We know that, early in his healing career he tried using charms and magic but gave them up. He also used a book of spells but burned it. It was also said that he was an admirer of the Christian mystic Jacob Boehme. These pursuits would certainly be poorly viewed by the church, and they take on more meaning in view of what certainly seemed to be Greatrakes' religious radicalism. Did he give up these things because he found they did not work or because he feared persecution? His real feelings remained a mystery.

And this brings us to the holy grail of the Greatrakes project—the diary. From the Hayman genealogy of the Greatrakes family, we knew that Greatrakes kept a diary. According to Hayman, the diary remained in the family for generations, into the early nineteenth century, when the manuscript was last known to be in the possession of Greatrakes' great-granddaughter Dorcas, of Youghal. In 1830, she gave it to her kin, and reportedly it became lost. Dorcas died in 1833. With the growing divide between the public and the private Greatrakes, the question of what this diary might contain became ever more important. Could it reveal his real thoughts and reflections? What became of the diary? Did it still exist? I shall come back to these questions later.

After an abysmally short stay in Lismore during our first trip to Ireland, Iain and I awoke to an early breakfast and headed for Affane: the Greatrakes land at last. We followed a road east for several miles along the Blackwater River to the town of Cappoquin, where we stopped to ask directions from two men standing on a corner. They looked as though they had been standing there forever. Wait a minute; we're in Ireland. Is this the origin of Samuel Beckett's *Waiting for Godot*? One of the men had what I can only call the gooniest of smiles. "Affane?" he said with a wide grin, revealing a mouth with more empty spaces than teeth. "It's just down there," he said, pointing south.

We pulled out of town with only a mile to go. Clearly not much had changed in the past three hundred years. No shopping malls, no housing developments, no golf courses. "Affane was never a village as Americans imagine it," Iain said. "There was never anything like a street with shops and so forth. That would have been Cappoquin. Affane was more like a large estate with a number of farmhouses."

Iain was right. There was nothing to tell the traveler that this was Affane, much less the Greatrakes land. Without our land survey maps showing us the precise location, we could have easily driven by.

Set back from the road was a cluster of barns next to a large farmhouse, the Greatrakes house. We walked up the service drive and found

Affane House, front view. A tree has sprung up in front of the entry to the house, which has been vacant for many years.

a man digging potatoes in a small plot of earth next to the house. It was Mr. O'Donnell, the owner of the land. He stood ankle deep in mud, wearing high rubber boots and an old overcoat held on by a piece of string tied around the waist. O'Donnell was a tall man with a craggy face and looked to be in his sixties. He had the intense look of a man who spent years alone and only seldom spoke. We introduced ourselves and told him we were looking for information about Valentine Greatrakes. "Greatrakes?" he said. "Oh, he's out in the barn!" Iain and I did a double take. "Greatrakes, in the barn?" "Sure," he said, "Greatrakes the horse!" We explained that we wanted a different Greatrakes, lived three hundred years ago, a healer, and so on. "Never heard of him," he said shaking his head.

O'Donnell had owned the house since the mid-1950s. He thought to fix it up and settle down with a family but never married and the house was never fixed up. With no upkeep, it was clearly in disrepair. "The last people to live here," he said, "were the Powers. Two brothers

Affane House. The rear section with no roof dates from the seventeenth century. The front wing was added on in the nineteenth century.

and a sister in their nineties. Never married." (We later learned that they were collateral descendants of the Greatrakes.) They lived here with five servants, also in their nineties. Everyone died within a few months of one another. In their final years, the brothers and sister made a deal with the local tax collector: Turn a blind eye to the property taxes, and the family would bequeath him the land, which they did. O'Donnell bought the land from the tax collector. "Nobody's lived in the house for a very long time," he said. "It's a terrible thing to see it go to ruin. It truly was a fine house. Would you boys like a look inside?" We walked around to the front of the house, a nineteenth-century Georgian style add-on to the much older rear section, which dated from what looked like the seventeenth century. The roof in the older section was gone. In Ireland, no taxes are owed on a house with no roof.

O'Donnell pushed open the wooden door. "I never lock it anymore," he said. "Vandals just break in, anyway." There is a kind of somber beauty to a grand old house that has gone to ruin. Despite the decay

Remains of the staircase in the entry of Affane House

and dilapidation, one can still feel the elegance and refinement of an era long since passed. Only the first four steps of the gracious circular staircase in the entryway remained. The rest had fallen away, leaving an ascending outline on the faded beige wall. The Greek columns that once graced the foyer had fallen through a large hole in the wooden floor and lay in the basement below. Their capitals still clung to the ceiling overhead. In the parlor sat an old grand piano covered with a thick coat of dust. The marble fireplace had been stolen, ripped out by scavengers and leaving a gaping hole in the wall. Scattered across the floor were large pieces of nineteenth-century hand-painted wallpaper.

Iain and I walked the grounds as Mr. O'Donnell went about his chores. In front of the house lay a large expanse of lawn and the faint outline of a path leading off to the old main gate to the house, dating back

Affane Church. Built in 1819 a few feet from the church where Greatrakes worshipped, it has been abandoned for many years.

to horse-and-carriage days. Running alongside the property was the Finisk River, no more than a large creek, a tributary of the Blackwater.

Iain and I walked down to the bank of the Finisk and saw the ruins of a large foundation, suggesting that a significant structure of considerable height had once stood here. As I mentioned earlier, Valentine manufactured lumber for export and maintained a brewery. Perhaps this structure was storage or holding quarters for goods waiting to be shipped out.

Across the road from the Greatrakes house stood a churchyard enclosed by an old wrought-iron fence. At its center was a church surrounded by grave markers and tombstones—a perfect setting for a Gothic novel. The iron gate to the churchyard squeaked as I pushed it open. The church Greatrakes worshipped in was torn down in 1819. This, the "new" church, was built in its place not long afterward and has long since been abandoned. The roof was gone and the bare stone structure was heavily overgrown with vines. Originally we thought Valentine was buried here, but then we learned that he was buried at the cathedral in Lismore. We walked through the tall grass, trying to make out names on the markers. Iain called out. "Leonard, come here, look at this!" He was bent over a tombstone, brushing the dirt and leaves aside. It was Greatrakes' grandson. The chiseled letters were worn but still readable: "Here lieth the body of Mr. Valentine Greatrakes, departed the seventeenth day of December 1759."

Iain pulled out the land survey map and pointed to the spot on the west side of the Blackwater, where Greatrakes' grandfather had built his castle in the 1580s. "Wonder if anything's there," he said. We drove north to Cappoquin to cross the river, doubled back a ways, and, after a few dead ends, found a dirt road running along the west river bank. We trundled past a row of trees, and suddenly, there it was, in the middle of a freshly plowed field. This was more than just foundation ruins. Whole sections of wall stood three storeys high. Through the heavy overgrowth clinging to the ruin, we could see windows, a doorway, a chimney.

Standing in front of the original Greatrakes house brought Iain and me face-to-face with one of the more puzzling and arcane questions of this history: At which of these two locations, the east or the west bank of the Blackwater, was Valentine born?

We know with certainty that the family first settled on this spot when grandfather William constructed this, his "fortified house," in the 1580s. At that time, this side of the river was called New Affane. We also know that the family later acquired land on the east bank, where they constructed the house we had just visited.

But in the reference material—be it *A Brief Account*, Greatrakes' personal correspondence, the family genealogy, or records of family wills—the accounts vary as to who was living on what land at what time. In *A Brief Account*, Greatrakes wrote that he lived in Affane, and so we assumed that he had been born in the house on the east bank. But in a letter written some months earlier in 1665, he made reference to his home being on the other side of the river, in the "fortified house." Greatrakes wrote that his father was from Affane. Hayman wrote that the father was from New Affane. Is it possible that Affane and New Affane were used interchangeably? *A Brief Account* was published in London for an English, hence a foreign, audience. Just as someone might say he or she is from Chicago when in fact the person is from a small town nearby, was Greatrakes really from New Affane, which he called Affane for a foreign audience? The results of this ambiguity leave us with the unsettling realization that, while this relatively small area is thick with history, there is no way of knowing with certainty in which of the splendid, imagination-inspiring ruins Greatrakes was born.

Iain and I walked down to the river's edge. A small rowboat tied to a pole bobbed in the water. "This is probably the very place where the Greatrakes pushed off from to cross to the other bank," Iain said. He pulled a notebook out of his shoulder bag and looked at his notes. "Of course, *affane* in Old Irish means 'middle ford.' There are three places on the Blackwater River that are fordable and this is the middle one, the middle ford." We stood quietly. It was August, and nature was in its fullest bloom. The water was still as glass. The dense green

Blackwater river looking north from the banks of Affane

foliage poured over the riverbank into the river. Wisps of fog hung inches above the water's surface like balls of cotton. Low-lying clouds streaked across the brilliant blue sky. In the intense quiet of this place with nothing at all to remind us that we were in the twentieth century, it was easy to imagine Greatrakes strolling up the path, greeting us, and walking by.

Later that afternoon, we phoned Evelyn the librarian at the county library to inquire about this land and the original Greatrakes house; we learned that the owner was Shane Jameson, of the Jameson Whiskey family. We phoned him the next day. When he learned of our interests, he said, "What? You're interested in the Greatrakes Castle! G'wan, I'll give it to ya, it's yours!" Iain and I are most pleased to be the owners of a castle in Ireland.

One of the more bizarre items we collected in our hunt was an article from an Irish journal stating that, in the 1640s, Greatrakes had tried to establish a new town at a place east of Affane. Greatrakes a city planner? "The streets were marked out and paved and several houses built which are since gone to ruin." The 1640s! Greatrakes was only born in 1628. The author of the article, a John Mulholland, attributed this information to "local tradition." What local tradition?

In 1990, a conflict in my and Iain's schedules sent me off to Great Britain without him. Not wanting to drive on the wrong side of the road, I enlisted Juliet, an old friend from my Paris days, to accompany me on the trip. We met at her home in Bristol, England, and drove to Ireland in her old French Citroen Deux Chevaux, the car that looks as though it were fashioned out of sardine cans.

Talking to John Mulholland was a must. We drove to Lismore to consult with Evelyn the librarian, who came up with his phone number. "Oh, I heard about it from Mickey Kent of Kilmacthomas," Mulholland said. "He owns a pub in town just opposite the Catholic church. Never gets there before six. You should stop by and see him if you want to know more. But I warn you, as pubs go, it's an odd place." "What do you mean odd?" I asked. "Oh, you'll see," he replied.

Kilmacthomas was about an hour's drive from Affane. A few miles before town, we picked up a hitchhiker, a gentleman in his seventies.

"We're going to a pub in Kilmacthomas, Mickey Kent's place," I said. "Do you know him?"

The man chuckled. "You're goin' to Mickey's place, are ya? Oh, you'll see."

We drove into the middle of town and stopped at the Catholic church. Our hitchhiker pointed across the street. "Well, there y'are," he said. "That's it over there." Opposite us stood a small, one-storey ramshackle building, but nothing that resembled a pub. Stuck in the window was a metal sign: CLOSED. The weather-beaten door was unlocked and open a crack. I peered inside. Just then, a gaunt man in his sixties walked up. Without saying a word, he shoved the door open and entered. Obviously Mickey. Stoop-shouldered and pale, he wore an old raincoat that looked as if it had been slept in for days. We peered in through the doorway and followed him inside. He switched on a naked lightbulb, and I immediately understood what everyone was talking about.

There had been a conflagration of some kind. The interior of the pub had been burned to a crisp. The walls and ceiling looked as if someone had given them a once-over with a flamethrower. The large mirror that hung over the bar was gone. All that was left was the empty wooden frame, blackened by smoke. On the scorched wall hung a shiny mandolin. Next to it, a cutout picture of Minnie Mouse and a charred picture frame empty of its contents.

The floor was a carpet of cigarette butts. Newspapers and magazines were stacked up in the corner, their edges singed black. The bar

Mickey Kent's bar, dusted off and in use again after the fire

itself was remarkably intact, burned but still in one piece. On a shelf in front of the former mirror sat an assortment of liquor bottles, gleaming among the sooty debris of the fire. Mickey poured himself a glass of milk and began lining up sparkling clean glasses on the bar. Just then, a group of young kids poured in through the door and the eerie interior filled with chatter. Not a word passed between Mickey and the youngsters. He stood sullenly behind the bar, busying himself washing glasses, and never looked up. Clearly, he didn't want to talk to anyone.

Then, as quickly as they came in, the youngsters finished their drinks, threw some money down on the bar, and departed. Mickey looked at Juliet and me. "You're not with them?" he said. "No," Juliet replied, "we just happened along at the same time." "Those bloody kids are from a neighboring town and only come here to see the strange old bird," he said. Mickey had a thick brogue and spoke haltingly with a barely audible voice. I moved closer. He told us about the fire some months back. No sooner were the flames out than he started pouring drinks again. "We let it air out a bit," he said. "Not too bad, huh?" "No, no, it's fine," Juliet said smiling.

My questions were pressing on my mind, but I wanted to warm up the conversation before getting to the meat of things. Mickey asked where I was from, and at the mention of San Francisco, his tired and drawn face flashed with animation. San Francisco was his favorite city in the world, he said, the one place he hoped to see before he met his Maker. There was a pause, and I made my move. "Have you ever heard of Valentine Greatrakes?" I asked. Mickey nodded yes and mumbled something barely intelligible. I moved my stool closer so as not to miss a word. Just then he reached under the counter and pulled out, of all things, a large model of a cannon and placed it on the counter directly between us. "You see this?" he said, his voice rising. "You know where this is from?" I was taken aback. "I don't know," I said. "It's from Saaaaan Fraaaaancisco!" he pealed. He flicked a switch under the barrel of the cannon. A radio snapped on, blaring out scratchy music. For the first time, Mickey smiled. "From Saaan Fraaancisco!" he said, cooing like a bird.

"Nice, really nice," I said. "But Valentine Greatrakes. Did you ever hear anything about him trying to start a new town around here?" Mickey nodded and said something, but I don't know what. The radio, plus his thick brogue and weak voice, made it impossible to understand him. He said something about the town hall at Carrick on Suir. "What was that?" I said, leaning closer, straining to hear. Just then, a couple

Jasper the grave digger, seen from the window of our car

of old regulars entered. They sat down at the bar, nodded to Juliet and me, and began conversing with Mickey. He poured them each a Guinness. The figures of these men, heavily shadowed under the stark light of the naked lightbulb overhead, their bent shapes, their craggy faces and rumpled coats, their stillness—they looked like something out of a painting, maybe Van Gogh's *The Potato Eaters*. Or was it one of Rembrandt's peasants? Timeless, in any case. Watching them absorbed in their own world, I felt as if I were on an ice floe about to go over the falls. I made an effort to get the conversation back, but it was no use.

On our way to Affane, Juliet and I got lost, so we stopped in Cappoquin to ask directions. We pulled up to two men standing on a corner. One of them was the same man Iain and I had asked directions from the year before. "Excuse me," I said, "we're looking for Affane. Can you help us out?" It was the man with the big, gooney smile. He peered into the car. "You're lookin' for Affane, are ya? It's becomin' quite the tourist site. C'mon, I'll take ya there!" He climbed into the backseat and we drove off.

Our voluntary guide introduced himself as Jasper. He made his living, among other things, he said, as a grave digger. "Someone dies, and I make a few bob," he said, chuckling. We were barely out of town when he began talking a blue streak. He had a strong, bubbly voice and clearly loved to talk.

We arrived at Affane and parked in front of the churchyard across from the Greatrakes land. In the year since my last visit, the grass had grown thick and was shoulder high. Many of the tombstones were lost in the overgrowth. Jasper led Juliet and me over to a corner of the churchyard, to an underground crypt that Iain and I had not seen before. A half dozen stairs led underground to a wooden door, barely hanging on its hinges. Jasper gave a shove and nodded toward the inside. "G'wan in," he said, grinning wide. Juliet and I descended the stairs slowly. The air grew cool and moist. We peeked inside. Two wooden coffins sat on a trestle. They had either been broken into or were decomposing with age. Their wrought-iron handles had fallen off and lay on the ground. Juliet pointed to a human thigh bone lying in the corner. "This place gives me the creeps," she said. "Can we please leave?" Jasper stood at the top of the stairs, chuckling.

We left the churchyard, crossed the road, and had hopped over the gate leading up the service drive when a bull nonchalantly rounded the corner of the barn and stood looking at us, his head held low. It suddenly occurred to us that hopping back over the gate would be a fine idea. We walked down the road to a spot where we could easily climb the fence. The embankment was covered with stinging nettles, and Juliet, with open-toed sandals, was reluctant to cross. Jasper bent down and with bare hands cleared aside the nettles. He then took her by the hand and helped her over the fence. As we walked across the expanse of grass approaching the Greatrakes house, Jasper suddenly began spouting poetry. "Her eyes are like the breeze, her hair the color of the trees, her beauteous visage . . ." "That's wonderful, Jasper," I said. "Whose poetry is that?" He beamed his toothless grin. "It's mine!" he said. "I made it up for the lady!" At that moment, the world stopped. If there is such a thing as the magical fringe, this was it. Here was a man from another time and another world. An uneducated man by modern standards, yet living in a world of art and poetry, a remnant of the ancient tradition of bards long since disappeared.

We found the front door to the house unlocked as usual. Things hadn't changed much. The grand piano was still in the parlor, perhaps covered with a bit more dust. More of the wallpaper was strewn on the floor. Sadly, scavengers had taken some of the lead off the roof, and the slate was loosening and beginning to fall off. Water was starting to leak in. Was this the end?

On the road back to Cappoquin, Jasper talked nearly nonstop. As we drove past a beautiful glen, he gazed out the window and fell into a poetic cadence. Juliet told him about our fantasy of rebuilding the Greatrakes house and turning it into a center, perhaps for the study of alternative medicine. Jasper smiled. "Oh, that's a good idea, indeed.

Make me one of the doctors, and I'll make a few bob!" He rocked with laughter. Back in town, we dropped him off at the corner, where his friend was still standing. "G'bye, Miss," Jasper said, extending his hand to Juliet. "Bye now," he said, patting me on the shoulder. We pulled away in the Deux Chevaux and must have looked like a strange flying machine with arms flapping out the windows on both sides as we waved good-bye.

CHAPTER 7

AND THIS BRINGS US TO Harold McCoy and the stolen harp. The strangeness of Greatrakes is matched here by another strangeness, this time one that is deeply American. Harold McCoy is from Arkansas. This is a detour, but it will quickly bring us back to Greatrakes.

Meg, an eleven-year-old girl living in Berkeley, played the harp. This was no ordinary harp, but a wooden harp hand-carved from a solid piece of bird's-eye maple in the style of the old Celtic harps. This one-of-a-kind gem, much loved by Meg, was like a member of the family. In 1991, the harp was stolen from a theater where Meg was performing in a series of concerts. The young musician was devastated. The police could turn up nothing and discouraged the family from getting their hopes up. Rare objects such as this are hardly ever seen again, they said.

For two months, her mother, Lisby Mayer, pursued every avenue to recover the harp: contacting instrument dealers across the country, running stories in the American Harp Society newsletter. CBS-TV even did a news story.

A call to Mayer's mother got some advice in addition to the expected sympathetic response. "Have you thought of trying a dowser?" she asked. "People say a good dowser can find lost objects from a distance." Mayer was skeptical yet asked, "Who's the best dowser?" "I don't know," her mother replied, "but I'll find out." A few days later, the older woman called Mayer. "Call Harold McCoy in Arkansas," she told Mayer. "If anyone can help, it's him." Mayer jotted down McCoy's phone number and, with nothing to lose, phoned him the next day. All she told him was that she had had a valuable harp stolen. No details about Meg, the concert, or anything else. McCoy asked only where it had been stolen. "Oakland," Mayer replied. "Send me a map," he said. Several days later, McCoy called back. "Well, I've located your harp."

While Mayer sat in her kitchen looking at a map of the Bay Area, McCoy sat in Arkansas looking at the same map and guided her to a location in Oakland. "Get off the freeway at the Ninety-sixth Street exit . . ." And so on, with the details of where to go. Astonishingly, he directed her to a specific location on a street. "It'll be the second house from the corner, on your left," he said.

The following morning, Mayer drove to the house in Oakland, but what could she do? She called the police, but without proof they could do nothing. Then she hit on an idea. She made up a flyer: STOLEN HARP,

REWARD, NO QUESTIONS ASKED, and put it up on phone poles within two blocks of the house.

Several days later, she got a phone call. The caller said he didn't have the harp, but that his next-door neighbor did. Without giving his own name or phone number, he said he would see to it that the harp was returned. Two weeks later, after numerous phone calls, the man arranged for Mayer to meet a teenage boy in the parking lot of an all-night supermarket, she with an envelope with the money and the boy with the harp. In an interesting twist, the caller did not demand a reward, but when Mayer asked how much money she should bring, he said, "My neighbor bought it for four hundred dollars. Would that be too much?" "Not at all," said Mayer. The harp, of course, was worth many times more. The meeting took place, and the next day Meg was a very happy young girl.

When I heard this story, it stopped me dead in my tracks. What can one say? Was this a fluke, a coincidence? Maybe it was plain luck. To make the inexplicable even more so, not long afterward McCoy located a source of water on Mayer's mother's farm in Vermont by dowsing only a map of the land.

A question came immediately to mind. Could McCoy find the Greatrakes diary? A couple of months after the harp incident, McCoy and his wife came to the Bay Area to visit relatives. Iain and I spent a morning with the couple, going over the Greatrakes saga and the tale of the lost diary. McCoy was interested in our story and had a strong feeling that the diary did exist, not in England or Ireland, but in Scotland, he said. He sensed that it was sitting in an old trunk, in an attic owned by people who did know they had this document. Sitting together, we watched as McCoy dowsed a map of Great Britain and pinpointed a location outside Edinburgh, in the town of Bathgate. A few weeks later, Iain obtained a map of Bathgate from friends in England and mailed it to McCoy.

Within several days, we received an envelope with the results of his latest dowsing. "If you stand at the east end of Starlaw Terrace and look west," he wrote, "it should be in the third or fourth house on the right."

Iain and I were now faced with a dilemma. The successful retrieval of the harp had enticed us as if we were gamblers hearing about someone hitting the jackpot in Las Vegas. Hmmm...maybe us, too. We pondered the situation. We had a trip coming up to England and Ireland, and a side trip to Bathgate would only mean an extra thousand miles and two days of driving. We decided to go there.

In preparation, we thought that a local news story in Bathgate about our search might jog some memories before our arrival. But did Bathgate have a newspaper? Iain phoned the Bathgate City Hall and learned there was indeed a paper, a weekly, the *Lothian Courier*. Next, he phoned the paper. Covering the mouthpiece, he whispered to me, "Better not mention healer, or dowser. Bathgate is Calvinist country, very pragmatic people. Healer, dowser, two guys from California? That would doom us before we started."

"Hello, this is Iain Boal. I'm calling from San Francisco." "*The* San Francisco?" chimed in the excited voice from the other end. "Yes, as a matter of fact it is," Iain replied. The woman was sufficiently intrigued by our story and agreed to write something in the next issue. "Good thing you called just now," she said. "We go to press in the morning."

From London, we sped along the M1 Highway in our small rental car like a mole going after its prey: quick and to the point. The drive through northern England and into Scotland was breathtaking. The December air was crisp and clean, the countryside rolled on forever. We arrived in Edinburgh late in the afternoon and went to the address of a friend of Iain's, who put us up.

The next morning at around eight we drove to Bathgate. Morning in this part of the world in the dead of winter is a desolate landscape indeed. The street we were looking for was part of a subdivision of houses no more than twenty-five years old and built on old farmland. The image of old houses lived in for generations by the same families, people who might have the diary and not know it, disappeared in a poof. Studying our local map, we found Starlaw Terrace. It was only seven or eight houses long, with the front doors opening on to a common. We parked the car and walked to the third and fourth houses. How strange we must have looked—two figures lurking about in the cold, dark, foggy morning, briefcases in hand, trying to see if anyone was stirring inside the houses. Not a soul in number three. We did see someone moving around in number four. OK. So we knock. Then what? What do we say? How about if I intone (arms outstretched à la Boris Karloff), "Good morning, madam, we've come for the diary"?

Iain knocked. A woman opened the door with an infant tugging on her apron. "Good morning, madam," he said. "My friend and I are doing a genealogical search and we thought that perhaps . . ." "Oh, is that so?" she said smiling broadly. "I saw you standing outside there and thought you were either Quakers, or double-glazed-window salesmen. Won't you come in for a cup of tea, then? I'll put a kettle on!" We deposited our briefcases in the foyer and stepped into an immaculate living room. "A genealogical search? Fancy that. Who is it you're looking for, anyway, if you don't mind my asking?" In a moment, Iain and I had our coats off and were seated on the couch with cups of tea in hand. The fireplace glowed with fake logs and flame.

Careful to avoid the H and D words, *healer* and *dowser*, Iain merely told the woman that we were researching the life of a mysterious seventeenth-century Anglo-Irish gentleman and had reason to believe that his diary, a most valuable document, was in this area of Bathgate. We did not say that her house had been pinpointed. My curiosity now was completely unbridled, irrational even. Like the person who becomes unhinged looking for the car keys and goes back to the same pocket over and over again while knowing he has just looked there, I began eyeing the place. I felt like a criminal casing the joint. Had I a crowbar, I would have started pulling up the floorboards.

"Oh, I'm quite sure we don't have anything like that here," the woman assured us. Iain inquired if there might be stored away in the attic some old family trunks that haven't been looked at for years. "We only moved here a few years ago," she said, "and there's not much at all in the attic. Sorry." Later that morning, we reached Mr. Donovan, the man at house number three. "Nothing like that around here." Click.

We then visited the offices of the *Lothian Courier* to see if the article had been published. Iain and I met the young editor, Morag Lindsay. She sat in a small room jammed with desks topped by computer terminals. The general mess of the office was the telltale sign of the ever-present deadline. Morag pulled out an old copy of the *Courier* and opened to our article. "Missing Link Sought" read the headline. The small article was buried on the page, and it was doubtful whether anyone really saw it. Iain and I conferred for a moment. There was only one thing to do now. Let the cat out of the bag—healer, dowser, the whole story. Create a sensation about this most valuable document so that people would think they're sitting on a winning lottery ticket. There was nothing to lose. Morag listened politely as we told her about Greatrakes healing cancer and leprosy, his being called before the king, Harold finding the harp, dowsing a map of Scotland, and on and on. She was thoroughly unfazed.

"You think it's a hoax, don't you?" asked Iain. Morag nodded yes. "It's the name," she said, "it's a dead giveaway." "The name?" I said. "Sure, Greatrix," she shot back. Of course. With the Scottish accent, *Greatrakes* is pronounced *Greatrix*, or "great tricks." Who would have thought? Luckily, I had my laptop computer with me and flipped it open to the numerous Greatrakes files. Morag leaned forward and gazed at the small screen as I scrolled through our bibliography of over one hundred entries, letters by Robert Boyle, accounts of cures, and other documents. She finally conceded and agreed to do another story, this time more prominently displayed, which she did. But the article appeared on Christmas Day. Does anybody read the newspaper on Christmas Day?

In the case of the stolen harp, I later learned that the house indicated by Harold McCoy was not the actual house where the harp was. Harold was keying into something, and that something was close enough to get the harp back. Maybe he was off here by a short distance, too. The old farmhouse that dominated the once-large farmland still stood; we could see it in the distance, and it was occupied. Unfortunately, our brutal schedule left us no time to investigate, and to this day, that farmhouse is the one stone left unturned in this story.

And now to *A Brief Account*. The impossible was about to happen. One day, I was in San Francisco, in the neighborhood of a rare book shop that specialized in the history of medicine, and thought to stop in. The idea of finding a copy of *the* book in my own backyard was so utterly preposterous that the thought never crossed my mind.

No sooner had I entered the shop than I felt my book endorphins set off. Among the shelves of medical works were other classics such as a first edition of Thomas Hobbes' *Leviathan* with a frontispiece by William Faithorne, the same man who did Greatrakes' portrait for *A Brief Account*. The pleasure of this bookshop was that while everything was neat and orderly, there was enough stock from floor to ceiling to give the feeling of being amid a massive jumble of books, and this surely increased the endorphins.

On a table sat a copy of the dealer's latest catalog. "Hmmm, let's see what he has." I picked it up and nonchalantly flipped through the pages. Then I froze. There it was in black and white—*A Brief Account*. Had anyone been looking at me at that moment, the observer would have seen the blood drain from my face. Calmly, I asked the proprietor if I could see the book. He was a short, slight gentleman with harmless eyes, graying hair, and a thoroughly languid manner. "Oh, I'm sorry," he said, "I just sold it." My heart sank. "Yes, it went to a man in Australia. But I may have another copy," he added. I was speechless. He explained that he had just bought a large library from a collector who specialized in the history of medicine and that he might have seen a copy there. "It'll take me weeks to sort through everything. Leave me your name and number, and I'll call you if I come across it."

Weeks and months went by with no word. I took it as a lost cause and forgot about it. Later in the year, I happened to be in the neighborhood again and stopped in. I casually asked the dealer if he had ever found the copy of the Greatrakes book. "Oh, yes, as a matter of fact I did," he said. "I've got it stored in the vault." I was aghast. Why hadn't he called me? With utterly perfect composure (inside I was a blithering

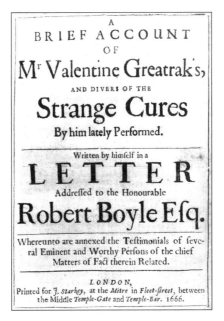

Title page from A Brief Account *by Valentine Greatrakes, 1666*

idiot), I followed this gentleman as he walked oh-so-very-slowly down a narrow corridor to the vault hidden away in a back room.

He pulled open the heavy steel doors of the vault and scanned the bookshelves. My eyes raced over the titles. I had already seen an original copy of *A Brief Account* and knew its size and shape. There it was! I pulled the slender volume off the shelf. To my dismay, the book I was holding was not *A Brief Account*, but rather an original copy of Henry

Stubbe's book, *The Miraculous Conformist*. The dealer casually reached up and pulled down not one, but two copies of *A Brief Account*. Did he have the David Lloyd book, too? "Oh, I'm sorry, I sold that one a couple of months ago." My pulse quickened.

With copies of *A Brief Account* and *The Miraculous Conformist* before me, I felt like Sidney Greenstreet gazing upon the Maltese Falcon. I was perspiring profusely. How much did these little items cost? I opened the Stubbe book and saw the price lightly written in pencil on the inside cover. More than any sane person would ever want to pay for a book. "I'll take it," I said. What was I doing? This was lunacy. We all have money put aside for a rainy day, but this was hardly a rainy day. I'd never pay more than a couple of dollars for a pair of socks, and now here I was, considering plunking down an outrageous sum for a book.

Of the two copies of *A Brief Account*, one was in pristine condition. It had been rebound by renowned bookbinder Bernard Middleton, and the pages had been washed and looked like new. The hand-tooled leather binding, newly done by Middleton, was exquisitely faithful to the period. The Faithorne portrait of Greatrakes sparkled with beauty and subtlety. The second copy was a hybrid version, with text pages from the original 1666 edition, but with a crude copy of the original Faithorne engraving. The binding was cheap and looked like something an amateur had done at home one evening in the person's spare time. The cost of the fine copy of *A Brief Account* would pay for a nice vacation to Europe. The less expensive copy was Europe on the cheap. Should I buy one? Which one? Why not both? No, impossible! I handed the two Greatrakes books to the dealer. "Can you hold these for me? I'm going out of town for a couple of weeks. I'll call you when I get back."

I was going on tour with my one-man show and would have plenty of time to ponder long and hard. Someone once said, "When the universe speaks, you'd better listen." Was the universe telling me something? Three copies of *A Brief Account* in San Francisco in less than a year. The odds were astounding. Whenever I went on tour, the first thing I'd do on reaching my hotel room was grab the Yellow Pages and look up the rare book sellers. Now, on this trip, as I traipsed from one shop to the next, I wondered what would become of me if I passed up the opportunity in San Francisco. For the rest of my life, I'd be this old geezer kicking around rare book stores. "Excuse me," I'd say, chomping on my false teeth, "have you ever heard of Valentine Greatrakes? *A Brief Account* . . . umm . . . 1666 . . . umm, he was a healer . . ."

The irony would be that one day I would find the book, and the dealer would say, "Why yes, we do have a copy. But you know, ever since that book was written about him some years ago, the price has skyrocketed. Frightfully expensive, I'm afraid." And I would have priced myself out of the action.

Two weeks after holding those rare books in my hands, I walked out of the San Francisco bookshop with my copy of *A Brief Account*, the finer edition. This, along with *The Miraculous Conformist*, gave me two out of the three pieces of the puzzle. Still missing was David Lloyd's

Wonders No Miracles. With my luck running so high, I was sure I'd find the book on some dusty bookshelf somewhere for only a few dollars.

Then something very strange happened.

In 1993, my theater in San Francisco, Life on the Water, produced a Saint Patrick's Day event. With my inclination for performing, I developed a stage monologue for the evening, telling Greatrakes' story as well as our own odyssey of unearthing his history. To publicize the performance, I made up a flyer, which I mailed to friends. Somebody—I never learned who—placed one of these flyers in the window of a café in the Potrero Hill district of San Francisco. A gentleman walking by saw the flyer and took notice. After the performance, he came backstage to introduce himself. His name was Bo Wreden, and he had startling news.

Until recently, his father, William P. Wreden, had been a rare book dealer in the town of Palo Alto, just south of San Francisco. In the 1950s, the elder Wreden had conducted research about Greatrakes with the idea of writing a book about him. The project was never completed. I felt as though I had just been told that I had a twin brother whom I had never met and who happened to be forty years older than me. My first thought was to meet Mr. Wreden, to compare notes. Sadly, I was too late. Although he was still alive, conversation was impossible. I asked Bo if Iain and I could see his father's bibliography. He was happy to help, but sorting through a lifetime of papers would take time, he said. We agreed to keep in touch.

A few days later, Bo called with the baffling news that the file of Gs from his father's papers was missing. The only thing he could find, he said, was a letter dated 1953 from his father's researcher in London. The letter told of his recent progress and the tediousness of sitting in the British Library for hours, and could Mr. Wreden please send more money. Then came the thunderclap. The name of Mr. Wreden's researcher in London was a Mr. Osborne. Mr. Osborne! Think back to *Notes and Queries* and the enigmatic 1953 letter written by the London man who was researching Greatrakes and was looking for the Greatrakes pamphlets owned by Mr. Gratix of Westpoint. This is the same Osborne!

The connection meant that the items Osborne had found, items that we had wondered about, would have ultimately ended up in Mr. Wreden's hands. My mind leapt to the cache of Greatrakes documents mentioned in *Notes and Queries*. Did Osborne find them? He did not, Bo said. At least he knew that much. How can we get ahold of Osborne? "Sorry, but he's passed on." In the weeks that followed, Iain and I managed to find Osborne's widow in England. She was not much help. After her husband died, she threw out all his papers except for a single box, which ended up on the TV and sat there for a number of years. She eventually threw those out, too.

A few months later, Bo phoned with the news that he had come across several more letters from Osborne and would send me photocopies. One letter in particular caught our attention. It began enthusiastically.

"News! I believe I have discovered a missing Samuel Mather manuscript relating to Greatrakes." Here was a document about Greatrakes that Iain and I had not come across, and from Samuel Mather! As noted earlier, Samuel Mather was the grandfather of Cotton Mather, of the infamous Salem witch trials in the 1690s. The Mather-Greatrakes connection was not unknown to us. We had come across a reference to Increase Mather, father of Cotton Mather, in a document dated 1684, in which he referred to Greatrakes as "the late miracle monger" who tried to cure an ague by using that "hobgoblin word, Abrodacara."

Unfortunately, Osborne did not say where he found the "missing Samuel Mather manuscript relating to Greatrakes." He effused over his find and was certain that it was "if not a literary discovery of major importance, at least a piece of Americana and Greatrakesiana of considerable interest." All the more tantalizing is Osborne's comment that he was working half an hour daily on transcribing and typing the manuscript.

But the best was yet to come. Several weeks later, Bo Wreden phoned me again. Sorting through his father's affairs, he discovered something fallen down behind a stack of Kate Greenaway books. It was a copy of the Lloyd book *Wonders No Miracles*. "Would you be interested in seeing it?" he asked.

The events that brought these books to me are mundane enough. Someone buys a book, and then for whatever reason, it leaves that person's hands; it then reenters the market and is sold once more.

Mundane, indeed. But that these books should find their way across the centuries and around the world to me in the Bay Area is a strange math indeed—the sum total of many small, ordinary acts adding up to something thoroughly extraordinary. I have never played the lottery, but it seems to me that I have faced the same odds and won.

EPILOGUE

*I*S THERE ANYTHING TO be learned from Valentine Greatrakes? To answer this question, we must look beyond Greatrakes himself. Iain and I worked on this project for eight years. Once in the throes of the work, I had no choice but to look at other phenomena I had witnessed in a new light.

Anomaly number one: On a trip to Sri Lanka in the early 1980s, I visited a small village far off the tourist track to watch a ritual of fire walking. For an entire afternoon, villagers stacked tree branches and coconut husks to a height of nearly six feet. The pile covered a surface about one hundred feet long and twenty feet wide. When everything was in place, liquid fuel was added and the entire pile was set aflame. Hours later, after the flames died down, the villagers used long, wooden poles to beat the embers into a flat, smooth surface. As darkness approached, hundreds gathered, drumbeats sounded, and the ritual began. By the dozens, men, women, and even young children approached the edge of this carpet of fire, discarded their sandals, and ran the length of it.

Having no way to understand this bizarre sight, I simply thought, well, they must be different, or maybe they had greased their feet beforehand and I just didn't see it, or some other rational explanation I missed. And with that, I slipped this experience into a convenient box and forgot about it.

Then, a few years later, a new fad appeared in the United States. Well-scrubbed, middle-class Americans gathered together in squeaky-clean Midwestern backyard patios to practice, of all things, fire walking. One of the strangest of human activities, once relegated to the world's most primitive cultures, had arrived in the American heartland. These people were not different, and I knew that no one was greasing his or her feet. Questions I had not asked myself in Sri Lanka leapt into my mind now. Have we not been taught that pain and the instinct to pull away are a universal response to fire? Are not the laws of nature immutable?

Anomaly number two: During the Christmas holiday of 1993, I gave a series of performances of my stage monologue on Valentine Greatrakes. One evening, two women, Elena and Thea, came to the performance and met me after the show. They knew each other, but neither had known the other would be coming that evening. It just so happened that a Russian healer was in Berkeley, staying at Elena's house. While we chatted, Elena invited Thea and me to come over and meet him.

The next day, about a dozen people gathered at Elena's house to meet Vladimir. Everyone sat in a circle, and after a short introduction in his less-than-perfect English, Vladimir stood before each of us, placing his hands a few inches from our face saying, "Feel the heat, feel the heat." Everyone acknowledged feeling the heat, except me. Although he held his hands in front of my face, I felt nothing and I told him so. He turned away for a moment, concentrated his attention, came back, and *whoosh!* I felt as if a hot iron had been placed in front of me. He then sat down and, in sequence, looked at each person in the circle, with his hands out in front of him as if he were picking up something about the person. Next, the Russian healer told people things about who they were, their ailments, things to look out for, and the like. When he came to me, he looked at me square on, his hands out in front of him, and said, "You are a healer. You don't know it, and you don't understand it, but you are a healer." There are not enough exclamation points in my computer to register my surprise at such a statement. In any case, to this day, I still don't know it and don't understand it.

But Vladimir's statement illuminated something else, something that happened to me at the very outset of this project. Until now, I have never told this to anyone. After the drive back from Stanford, when Iain and I sat at the café and shook hands, agreeing to take on this project, I had a most strange experience. Just as we shook hands, I felt my right arm shoot back over my shoulder and reach off behind me into the distance and touch Greatrakes' hand. Strange in the extreme, yes. At that moment, I thought it was strange and I still think it's strange today.

But there it was. I am not prone to things of this nature and have never had an anomalous experience before. If one wonders how I knew it was Greatrakes, I don't know. I just knew.

But the most significant part of the afternoon with Vladimir took place after the group had broken up and people were socializing. Vladimir took Thea aside into a room alone. He first washed his hands and then asked her to stand opposite him. From several feet away, he scanned her body, holding his hands out in front of him. He told her that she had breast cancer. He pointed to a specific spot on her left breast. Needless to say, she was alarmed. "But you will be fine," he said. If he's a healer, why didn't he heal her? I cannot answer this. I must add that Vladimir took no money from anyone that day. Thea went to the doctor, but the first examination, which included a mammogram, found nothing. Only after several subsequent procedures was a very small tumor found at the very spot Vladimir had indicated. Treatment was undertaken, and years later, Thea is fine. What an interesting confluence of events that had brought Thea and Elena to a performance about a healer and led Thea to a real healer who had such impact on her life.

Anomaly number three: In 1976, a handful of sailors from the small Pacific island of Satawal sailed their outrigger canoe twenty-five hundred miles from Hawaii to Tahiti, using no instruments of navigation. They carried no maps, compass, radar, or depth finder on board. Pialug, the captain, knew the winds, the currents, the swells of the ocean. He also knew the star coordinates and the distances between islands. All the information essential to the voyage he held in a chant, which he had memorized and then sang to himself to keep the canoe on course.

Young boys on Satawal are taught how to navigate by lying on their backs on the ocean for hours until they grow sensitive to the subtlest swells. This refined kinesthetic awareness of the sea can, at times, prove more important to survival than eyes. Some of the most famous navigators are said to have been blind.

Accompanying Pialug on his journey was an American colleague, a traditional navigator. In a film recording of the voyage, one can see the two men seated next to each other on the rail of the outrigger. Their physical demeanor speaks volumes about the cultural differences between them. Pialug can only be described as inordinately relaxed. His eyes are half closed, his jaw hangs loose, his motions are slow and deliberate. The American is alert, ferretlike, tense, searching. His countenance suggests an intellect that is engaging nature, processing data. Pialug looks like a sponge soaking up information through his senses. He gains knowledge through physical sensation, and this knowledge is embedded in his body. The American processes knowledge primarily through books and mechanical devices and retains information within his mind. Clearly, there are different ways of knowing. Pialug demonstrated that it is possible to gain precise knowledge through ambiguous means.

Beyond the intrinsic value of these anomalies, their enduring value lies in the challenge they present to our way of seeing the world. It is a simple challenge—to remain open. The knee-jerk reaction to reject outright anything that cannot be explained within the limits of our rational worldview limits us more than instructs us. Our world is reduced rather than made larger. Many people, I am sure, fear that to step outside the framework of Western rational thinking would lead us directly into an irrational world of ghosts, hobgoblins, witches on broomsticks, flying saucers, leprechauns, and every other manner of strangeness.

An exception is acupuncture. What could be stranger than performing brain surgery on people who are awake but who feel no pain because of anesthesia accomplished by the insertion of acupuncture needles around the eyebrows? Who would think that a kidney ailment can be treated by placing needles in the ears? After years of being viewed as so much voodoo, acupuncture is now accepted in the United States. Yet not everyone is convinced. When I told a skeptic that I had been successfully treated for a bothersome condition by acupuncture, she replied, "If you believe that, you'll believe anything." Dowsing fares worse. A person to whom I told the harp story surmised that Harold McCoy must have known the thief who stole the harp.

Trying to understand these anomalous phenomena is made more difficult by the frauds and fakes in the world. While the charlatans must be exposed, professional debunkers such as James Randi, aka Amazing Randi, with his blanket disavowal of anything that has the faintest odor of the so-called paranormal, do little good. I was impressed with his knowledge of Greatrakes until Randi wrote that the Irish gentleman had "accumulated a fortune" through his healings. Randi goes even further and makes Greatrakes a historical linchpin by asserting that Greatrakes helped "establish the precedent for modern healers." There is no truth to this.

Our language, full of prejudice, does not help. Just as *pagan* demeans any religion outside the Judeo-Christian tradition, words such as *paranormal* and *extrasensory* give anything they are attached to a weird aspect. The term *folk medicine* is equated with old wives' tales and quaint superstitions to which premodern people clung helplessly until the arrival of "official medicine."

Life is big. The world is big. The human mind and spirit are big. Why engage in behavior and ideas that diminish us? It is up to us to discriminate, to distinguish the real from the unreal. Because we are so quick to reject anything we cannot understand, we lack even the most basic questions that might lead us to an understanding of what is happening. Consequently, we are thrown back onto questions that only demean.

In a study some years ago, it was established that premature babies lying in their incubators grow healthier faster when they are touched and stroked. The mystery is not that this would be true, but rather that this is not common knowledge. The phenomenon of touch, contact, and other human connections are little understood and even less investigated. Despite the advances in unraveling the mysteries of human functioning, an understanding of what takes place in this simple action of touch is still distant.

When I was a schoolboy, it was believed that only humans had the intelligence to make tools. The phrase "Man the Toolmaker," an expression outmoded today, was bandied about like a clarion call hailing the arrival of these stalwart beings who had ventured so far, over such difficult terrain, to achieve this superior level of evolution. Then, a new generation of researchers observed more carefully. They abandoned old notions of hierarchy; they asked more probing questions and turned an old concept upside down. Animals, too, it turns out, make tools. New knowledge pushes on the boundaries of our small, unassailable world, and we are forced to redefine ourselves. Our knowledge of ourselves is, if anything, ephemeral.

Confronting the unexplainable, be it Greatrakes, Harold McCoy, Vladimir, or the Satawal islanders, it is worth recalling the motto on the title page of *The Miraculous Conformist*. "Because the obscure cannot be understood, does not mean the obvious should be denied."

APPENDIX

**In this excerpt, Valentine Greatrakes writes to the
Bishop of Chester, explaining how he came to his
healing talent, August 1666.**

My L[ord]

Some three years since I had an impulse (which sleeping or waking
in private or public) always suggested to me, I have given thee the
power of curing the King's Evil, which impulse, I a long time con-
cealed. At last (being in a manner haunted) I told my wife thereof,
whose answer was that I had conceived a rich fancy, and laughed at
the conceit. But it pleased God two or three days after, that there came
to my house the son of one Lem Mayher of the parish of Lismore

189

Testimonials from A Brief Account. *One of the witnesses is Robert Boyle.*

wherein I live, who had the Evil grievously in his eye, throat and face, desiring my wife to put some plaster to it, who told me of it, whereon I went with her to the person infected, and when I saw it was the Evil I told her, she should now be satisfied whether the impulse were a fancy of my own conception, or the dictates of god's spirit on my heart.

And thereon I laid my hands on the sores and swelling, desiring the Lord in mercy to heal the person. And afterwards that which was ... in hand ... within two days grew soft, then it ran, and within 3 weeks was perfectly whole and so continues (blessed be the Lord) to this day, being 3 years and upwards since.

After this, there came unto me (Dr. Anthony being at my house) a poor woman, a neighbor that had the Evil 7 years, and had it in 36 or 37 [different] places, whereon I desired the Doctor to take commiseration on her, and not to do all things for money, but somewhat for God's sake. His answer was that she was eaten out and all the men in Ireland could do her no good. I replied that there was certainly one man, that (through the power of God) could and would cure her. He asked his name. I replied it was myself, and . . . about 6 weeks afterwards, the doctor came to my house to see my wife, and the poor woman came also with a case of hazelnuts, and was perfectly well. And so several [others] from that time came to me that were infected with the disease and were healed.

Some two years afterwards, the Ague was almost epidemic in these parts. I had the same impulse (that God had given me) the gift of curing the Ague. Within a day or two, one came to me, and I put my hand on him, desiring the Lord to free him from it, and he heard my prayers, and so many were cured in like manner, their shakings immediately leaving them day after day. Soon after I had an impulse, I have given thee the gift of healing, and within three or four days afterwards, going to see a friend, there were several [people] that labored under several diseases, who desired me to lay my hands on them, who were immediately cured, and struck with amazement to see these diseases fly from place to place, and (like wildfire) run through them. And (in truth) it was as strange to me (being in another county) how they should come to the knowledge, that I (through Gods' mercy) could cure them, as that God had given me the gift to do it. Sir, God pleases by the touch at my hand to cure some and not others for which I can give no more reason more than that I should cure any. Those diseases which I seldom fail of curing, are the falling sickness, the King's Evil, the Ague, pains of most sorts, the gout often, and most obstructions.

[I] am but a worm, and cannot but stand amazed at the wonderful hand of God in these things. Sir, how long this gift may last, is a query that God only can answer. . . . I am Sir, your most humble and faithful Servant.

Valentine Greatracks

Eyewitness Accounts of Cures *from* A Brief Account

A woman's sight was restored.

I Margaret Westley of the Parish of Christ Church, London, do certify whom it may concern, that I have been almost blind of one of my eyes near twelve months, and have been with [many] persons to get cure, but could get none. But now under God I have received perfect cure by the stroke of Mr. Greatrak's hand. Which I testify to be true, and have subscribed my name, May 17. Anno Dom. 1666. Margaret Westley
Witnesses hereunto, John Owen of Bread Street, London, Math.
Porter, John Grone, William Faithorne.

John Harrison, skeptical of Greatrakes' powers, had to be persuaded to be stroked.

There being a report of Mr. Valentine Greatrak's who did cure all diseases by his hand, although I could scarce believe that an innate and an inborn disease could be cured, yet I was persuaded to go to him upon the certificate of one man who did inform me that he did cure him. . . . [My] Being born with the King's Evil (as they call it) . . . my parents did always endeavor a cure from the surgeons. They by their skill did prove its obstinacy by their repeated endeavors, and did break the node which was contracted in my right arm pit, and likewise another in my little finger of my right hand, but as I grew in strength, the disease grew more daring, and approached my throat, my face, and eyelids. . . . I made my address to him, who did freely stroke that part, as likewise my face, which touch did humble the swelling under [my] ear, and break it after it had troubled me by its soreness for 2 or 3 hours.

From his stroke the disease was beaten down into my small guts, and did pain me so extremely for 14 days. I endeavoring to cure it by other means, was persuaded it was the disease flew thither for refuge, which I found true, for going to him and he rubbing of it with his cold hand (an improbable means, as most do think) he, by this motion of his hand, did produce such a heat as did burn up all the pain.

But at this and the other times he stroked me I had such a sickness upon me as men have when they are about to vomit, and one time I vomited an acid frothy matter with some undigested phlegm. After this, viz, on Easter Monday I found some of this humor steal into my right leg, and was stroked there and it vanished. . . . When myself, or anyone else did tell him of the ease they received, I heard no vaunt in his language, but joyfully he said either "praised be God" or, "the glory be to God.". . . For his being an impostor as some have censoriously averred . . . his liberality will disprove. . . .

Present when Mr. John Harrison in Southwark wrote and
subscribed his name hereunto, Albert Otto Faber, M.D.
Memorand. That I was an eyewitness of Mr. John Harrison's
subscribing and owning of this certificate, George Weldon.

A woman was treated for breast cancer.

APRIL 10, 1666

Dorothy, the wife of John Pocock of Chiveley, in the county of Berkshire, aged 45, had a tumor began in her breast about August 1665, which in the beginning of April 1666 was grown so big as a large pullett's egg, and [thought] by sundry physicians and surgeons to be a cancer, and no other way of curing then by cutting it out, was twice stroked by Mr. Greatraks, and after the second time the tumor was grown softer so that he opened it, and out thereof flowed a great quantity of concocted matter, and after that by gentle stroking Mr. Greatraks brought forth the bag wherein the matter had lain, out of the small orifice, and she professes herself to be very well of her breast, and also to be freed of a great pain which she had had in her arm and shoulder for the space of eight months . . . past.

In the presence of Dorothy Pocock, Andrew Marvel,
J. Faireclough, Thomas Allured, Thomas Pooley

Excerpts from Personal Correspondence about Greatrakes

This letter from George Rust to Joseph Glanvill, March or April 1666, was written while Greatrakes was in London.

The great discourse now at the coffee-houses, and everywhere, is about Mr. G., the famous Irish Stroker. . . . He undergoes various censures here. Some take him to be a conjurer, and some an impostor, but others again adore him as an apostle. I confess, I think the man is free from all design, of a very agreeable conversation, not addicted to any vice, nor to any sect or party, but is, I believe, a sincere Protestant. I was three weeks together with him at Lord Conways and saw him, I think, lay his hands upon a thousand persons; and really there is something in it more than ordinary. But I am convinced it is not miraculous. I have seen pains strangely fly before his hand, till he has chased them out of the body, dimness cleared and deafness cured by his touch. Twenty persons at several times, in fits of the falling sickness, were in two or three minutes brought to themselves, so as to tell where their pain was, and then he has pursued it, till he has driven it out at some extreme part . . . but yet I have many reasons to persuade me, that nothing at all of this is miraculous. He pretends not to give testimony to any doctrine, the manner of his operation speaks it to be natural, the cure seldom succeeds without reiterated touches, his patients often relapse, he fails frequently, he can do nothing when there is any decay in nature, and many distempers are not at all obedient to his touch, so that I confess,

I refer all his virtue to his particular temper and complexion. I take his spirits to be a kind of elixir and universal ferment, and that he cures as (Dr. M. expresses it) by a sanative contagion.

(MARJORIE NICOLSON, *THE CONWAY LETTERS*)

Alexander Herbert Phaire, son of Greatrakes' close friend Robert Phaire, wrote this letter on March 10, 1743.

When Mr. Greatrakes came to my father's, the court was crowded with patients, whom he attended all the forenoon. Many were perfectly cured without any return of their disorders, and most received benefit. But in my time his virtue was much abated. I have heard my two eldest sisters (who were women grown) and my eldest brother, and my father and mother, and many other honorable people, that would speak nothing but truth, often say, that they have many times seen him stroke a violent pain from the shoulder to the elbow, and so to the wrist and then to the top of the thumb, and by holding it strongly there for sometime, it had evaporated. There are many wonderful relations of this kind, which tho' assuredly true, have so much the air of romance that I have no pleasure in relating them.

(BIRCH COLLECTION)

Abraham de la Pryme wrote about how Greatrakes' healing abilities were tainted by his helpers' taking payment for the stroking.

I was talking with this gentleman likewise about Greatrix, the famous Irish stroker. He says that he knew him very well, and lodged over the way just [opposite] him in London. He has talked with him several times, and says that he seemed to be a strange conceited fellow, believing strange things of devils, spirits, and witches, etc. He says he fancied him himself to be an impostor. He had two or three young men waiting upon him, who always pumped the persons that were going to be stroked, how long they had their distemper, whether they thought their master could cure them, etc. He never took one farthing for any cure that he did, nor would suffer his servants to do the same. But those that were cured, out of gratitude, a good while after, presented him and his servants with anything that he or they stood in need of. While this gentleman lodged over [opposite] him, which was for about three weeks, there was brought unto him near one hundred people, of which he says there was not over fifteen of them cured, upon which some people took notice thereof to him, "are they not so," says he. "I thought they had been all cured. Either they want faith, or some of my men has received money." So he called up his men, who having heard what was said, — "Sarrah, you rogues," says he, "some of you, I believe, has made my cures ineffectual by your rogueries. John, James, Thomas, Macko. Matko," says he, "I find you are the rogue that has received some of the poor's money, tell me?" So he confessed it. "Well," says he, "get you gone,

I'll make an example of you." So he went down. And the next morning the stroker and all his men went out of town. Thus this gentleman told me word for word. He saw this fellow at my Lady Conway's likewise, and does confess that he did by some way or other strange cures there. But there were several likewise that he could not cure.

(C. J. JACKSON, ED., *THE DIARY OF ABRAHAM DE LA PRYME*, 90–91.)

George Walsh, in a letter to his cousin Henry Slingesby, April 1666, was skeptical of Greatrakes.

I can tell you little of the stroaker that is worth the writing. Some say they are better for his stroking, others are worse. The King is far from having a good opinion of his person or cures. Printed books talk things of him, that I have not yet taken the pains to read.

(GRAHAM MANUSCRIPTS)

Mary Marshall, in a letter to the Reverend Mr. Joseph Boyle, recollected cures she saw Greatrakes perform many years earlier.

DUBLIN, MAY 2, 1699.

Sir,

As to Mr. Gratrix's cures, because I was not willing to trust too much to my own memory . . . it being near 20 years since I saw him stroke any[one] I have not written of any [except that] I have still some friends living who were eye witnesses as well as myself with whom I have compared notes yesterday to give you nothing here but what they think exactly true.

The first I shall mention was my own brother John Denison which both my sisters and myself well remember to have been seized with a violent pain in his head and back when about 14 years of age. One of my sisters at that time had the smallpox and my mother judging that he was taking the same distemper used no means to remove it till by accident Mr. Gratrix coming to our house and [hearing] of his illness desired to see him. He ordered the boy to strip him to his shirt, which he did, and having given him present ease to his head by only stroking it with his hands . . . but the pain immediately fled from his hand to his right thigh. He followed it there, it fell to his knee, from there to his leg, but he still pursued it to his ankle, then to his foot and last to his great toe.

As it fell lower it grew more violent especially when in his big toe it made him roar out, but upon rubbing it there it vanished and the boy cried out tis quite gone. It never troubled him after, but he took up smallpox about 3 weeks after.

I had also a comrade, one Mrs. Lile who after a fever was much troubled with a pain in her ears and [was] very deaf. She came to Mr. Gratrix's when at my father's. I remember he put some of his spittle into her ears and turning his finger in her ears rubbed and chafed them well which cured her both of the pain and deafness. Mr. Hartlies daughter-in-law, Mrs. Scrivenon, told me herself that she was, when a child, extremely troubled with the king's evil her mother sent her to be stroked in King Charles the 2nd and time to London but she was nothing the better, but Mr. Gratrix perfectly cured her.

I could add many things of this nature both of what I have seen and heard from my mother who was much more with him than myself. But wanting room shall only tell you that when he stroked for pains he used nothing but his dry hand. If ulcers or running sores, he would use spittle on his hand or finger, and for the evil if they came to him before it was broke he stroked it and ordered them to poultice it with boiled turnips and so did every day till it grew fat for lancing, he then lanced it and with his fingers would squeeze out the cores and corruption and then in a few days it would be well with his only stroking it every morning. Thus he cured many who keep well to this day. . . . I have been tedious and therefore shall not add but that I am your humble servant.

Mary Marshall

(STOWE COLLECTION)

This ballad was written in defense of Greatrakes.

❧ *Rub for Rub: or An Answer to a Physician's Pamphlet Styled, The Stroker Stroked* ❧

Come hither, Doctor, and behold in short
Something of truth, Sir, touching your report.
You with your beastly stories would delude
The Faith and Wisdom of the Multitude.

Ha, ha, Physician, is your envy such:
Are you so touchy, yet not brook a touch
You play'd the Poet but wer't much deceiv'd
To think your Fictions would be believ'd.
We laugh and scorn thy envious Libel, pish,
'Tis but the Froath of Malice, Womanish.
Whip behind Coachman, crys this envious Boy
Because he cannot, what that doth enjoy.
You envy't as his Happiness, and grutch
Because you cannot grope where he doth touch:
Doctor, your Practice is too scant I trow
Which makes you wound (anothers Credit) so,
And so you're in an Error most profound,
For he in Duty ought to Heal, not Wound
Alas, his Craft he cannot always smoother,
We see he doth the one as oft as th' other:
Doctor, you could not when you would defame,
You look't asquint, Sir, and so miss'd your aim.
True, you strook high, but wound you were not able,
For what you strook at was invulnerable.
Twas a Consumption in the Purse, I fear,
That made the Remedy, prescrib'd a Jear.
As once Demetrius fearing loss of Gain
Strove to confound what Heav'n did maintain.
Alas you fear your Craft would come to nought,

Because such Wonders by his Hands are wrought,
His Deeds pronounce his Worth: But let us know
What Honour we, to you Physicians owe.
We're not beholding unto you I'm sure,
Not you, but 'tis our Money gives us Cure,
Ye're Rhetoricians in our Cure, We see
'Tis wholly done by a Synecdoche.
Some Griefs you thoroughly Cure, and thy are these;
A rich mans Golden Plurisie finds ease.
And presently you Cure, as t'were by flight,
A heavy-hearted Purse and make it light.
Doctor, your Art to every Grief extends,
But yet you do your Cures for your own ends.
A friend of mine to prove the Doctor came,
And brought a Glass of Urin in's own name.
He took the Glass, he shak'd it, then reply'd,
A Fever strong, but saith the Doctor ly'd.
A Doctor for a Horse I swear he is,
The feav'rish Urin was a Horses Piss.
And by this instance, we may plainly see,
you're the Deceiver, Doctor, and not he.
Then he's a Jesuit, but you're in the wrong:
Physician. Cure thy self thy Tongue's too long.
Rather than nought, the very Truth you'l slander,
the Doctor's want of Practice makes him maunder.

But yet his envious Fictive Brain's not able,
To droll Reality into a Fable.
His hand is truly powerful whose stroke
Twice disposseth and made the Devil smoak.
What if he clip'd and clap'd, what's that to you?
You've clip'd and clap'd, and have been clap'd too.
For, if to me my author have not ly'd,
Though not, o'th' back, he once was Scarifi'd
Your foul report betrays you, and in truth,
I fear the Doctor hath a liquorish tooth.
Her Stocking off, he strokes her Lilly-foot,
What then? The Doctor had made a minde to do't.
Her Legs, her Knees, her Thighs, a little higher.
And there's the Doctors Center of Desire;
whereas he, as I for certain understand,
Hath searched many a wenches Country-land.
One Wench, I hear, and her disease was this,
And that no strange one is, the Green-sicknesse,
He saw the Maid was in a needy mood,
He strait presum'd a Clyster might be good:
He lays her on the bed, O beastly story!
And then thrusts in his long Suppository,
And tells her on his Faith deny't who can,
Nothing so good for her, as th'Oyl of Man.
And then I'm sure, if what is true, we're spoke,

She gave him tuch for tuch, and stroke for stroke.
But passing this, and many o'th' like sort,
Doctor, your Practice hath no good report;
And all suppose by your obscene Narration,
Your Brains and Back want a severe Purgation,
Your Pamphlet false, Reason it self implyes,
For t'was all Poetry, and therefore Lyes.
Thus you and I upon the Matter Strike,
You give a Rub, and I Return the Like.

VALENTINE GREATRAKES
CHRONOLOGY

12 February 1628 Born at Affane. Attends the Lismore Free School, which was erected for the Protestants by Richard Boyle, the Great Earl of Cork.

1632 Greatrakes' father, William, dies.

October 1641 Irish rebellion breaks out. Greatrakes' mother, Mary Greatrakes, flees to England with her children.

1642 English civil war breaks out. Oliver Cromwell leads revolt against the monarchy.

1646 or 1647 Valentine returns to Ireland to repossess the family lands lost during the rebellion. Depressed by the carnage, he goes into seclusion at Cappoquin for about one year.

1648 English civil war ends. Cromwell defeats the Royalists. English monarchy abolished. Greatrakes comes out of seclusion and joins Cromwell's army in Ireland to put down the insurgents. Greatrakes petitions for return of the family lands.

29 January 1649 King Charles I beheaded. Cromwell is new head of state.

1656 Greatrakes discharged from the army. Returns to Affane to rebuild his estate. Is appointed to civic positions: clerk of the peace for County Cork, and register for transplantation.

1658 Cromwell dies.

1660 British monarchy is restored. King Charles II returns to London. Greatrakes loses his civic positions because of his association with Cromwell.

April 1661 Greatrakes receives royal pardon for his part in Cromwellian wars in Ireland.

September 1661 Appears as an amateur witch finder at the trial of Florence Newton in Youghal.

1662 Experiences his first "impulse." Begins healing the king's evil. The Royal Society is founded.

1664 Greatrakes experiences his second "impulse."

April 1665 Experiences his third and final "impulse."

January 1666 Greatrakes brought to England by Edward Conway.

February 1666 Henry Stubbe writes *The Miraculous Conformist.* Greatrakes summoned to London by King Charles II.

13 March 1666 David Lloyd writes *Wonders No Miracles,* attacking Greatrakes.

April 1666 Greatrakes meets Robert Boyle in London.

8 May 1666 Greatrakes writes *A Brief Account* to vindicate himself.

June 1666 Returns to Ireland.

September 1666 The Great Fire of London.

1668 Visits England a second time.

April 1670 Dines with William Penn.

1672 Visits England a third time.

28 November 1683 Dies in Ireland at age fifty-five; is buried at Lismore Cathedral.

BIBLIOGRAPHY

Additional MSS. 60220, fol. 18v. Muggletonian Archives, British
 Library, London.

Add. MSS. 4182, fol. 29v–30. British Library, London.

Analecta Hibernica 15 (November 1944), 17 (1949) and 30 (1982).

Appleyard, O. B. "A Seventeenth Century Healer: Valentine
 Greatorex, 1628–1683." *Practitioner* 182 (March 1959).

Arnold, Lawrence J. "Valentine Greatrakes: A 17th Century 'Touch
 Doctor.'" *Eire Ireland: A Journal of Irish Studies* 11 (spring 1976).

——— . "The Irish Court of Claims of 1663." *Irish Historical Studies*
 24 (November 1985).

Aubrey, John. *Brief Lives*. Edited by O. L. Dick. Ann Arbor:
 University of Michigan Press, 1957.

Bagwell, Richard. *Ireland Under the Stuarts*. Vol. 3. 1885; London:
 Longmans & Co., 1909.

Bailey, Francis. *An Account of the Revd. John Flamsteed*. London, 1835.

Barnard, T. C. "The Hartlib Circle and the Origins of the Dublin
 Philosophical Society." *Irish Historical Studies* 19 (1974).

Beecher, Lyonell. *The Great Cures and Strange Miracles Performed by
 Greatrux, Mr. Valentine since his coming out of Ireland to the City
 of London*. Youghal, Ireland, 1666.

Birch Coll., Add. MSS. 4293, fol. 50–53; and Add. MSS. 4291.
 British Library, London.

Bodleian, MS. Carte 156, fol. 15–16.

Bottigheimer, Karl S. "The Restoration Land Settlement in Ireland: A
 Structural View." *Irish Historical Studies* 68 (March 1972).

Boyle, Robert. *The Works of the Honourable Robert Boyle*. Edited by
 Peter Shaw. London, 1778.

Braithwaite, William C. *The Beginnings of Quakerism*. London:
 Macmillan & Company, 1912.

Buckley, James. "Valentine Greatrakes: Selection from General Account Book of Valentine Greatrakes A.D. 1663–1679." *Journal of the Waterford and South East Archeological Society* 11 (1908).

Burns, Elinor. *British Imperialism in Ireland.* Dublin: Workers' Books, 1931.

Butler, George. "The Battle of Affane." *Irish Sword* (Journal of Military History Society of Ireland, Dublin) 8, no. 30 (1967).

Calendar of State Papers, Relating to Ireland, 1586–1588; 1586–1588; 1588–1592; 1599–1600; 1660–1662; March–October 1600; 1663–1665; 1663–1665; and 1666–1669. Ireland.

Cambridge University Letter, C.U.L. Add. MS. 1, no. 26. British Library, London.

Carthage (Father, O.C.S.O.). *The Story of Saint Carthage.* Dublin: Brown and Nolan, 1937.

The Civil Survey, County Waterford, A.D. 1654–1656. Dublin: 1942.

Coker, Matthew. *A Short and Plain Narrative.* London, 1653.

——— . *A Prophetical Revelation Given from God himself unto Matthew Coker.* London, 1654.

——— . *A Whip of Small Cords.* London, 1654.

Coleman, J. "Colonel Phaire, the Regicide." *Journal of the Cork Historical and Archeological Society* 22 (1914).

Crawfurd, Raymond. *The King's Evil.* London: Oxford Clarendon Press, 1911.

Critchley, Macdonald. "The Malady of Anne, Countess Conway: A Case of Commentary." *King's College Hospital Gazette,* 1937.

Crossley, James, ed. *The Diary and Correspondence of Dr. John Worthington.* Manchester: Chetham Society, 1855.

"A Detection of the Imposture of Mr. V. G. and his Pretended Gift of Healing." Sloane, 1926, fols. 1–10. British Library, London.

Dewhurst, Kenneth. *Dr. Thomas Sydenham: His Life and Original Writings.* London: Wellcome Historical Medical Library, 1966.

Douglas, John. *The Criterion; or, Miracles Examined with a View to Expose the Pretensions of Pagans and Papists*. London, 1754.

Dublin Penny Journal 1, no. 31 (January 26, 1833), and 1, no. 51 (June 15, 1833).

Duffy, Eamon. "Valentine Greatrakes: The Irish Stroker; Miracle, Science, and Orthodoxy in Restoration England; Religion and Humanism." *Studies in Church History* 17 (1981).

Edwards, R.W. D., and M. O'Dowd. *Sources of Early Modern Irish History*. Cambridge: Cambridge University Press, 1985.

Egan, P. M. *History, Guide and Directory of the County and City of Waterford*. Waterford, Ireland, 1894.

Field, T. Lindsay. *The Illustrated Guide to the Blackwater and Ardmore*. Youghal, Ireland, 1898.

Firth, Charles. *The Regimental History of Cromwell's Army*. Oxford: Oxford University Press, 1940.

Fleetwood, John. "Greatrakes the Stroker." *Ireland's Own* magazine, April 27, 1990.

———. *History of Medicine in Ireland*. Dublin: Brown and Nolan; Richview Press, 1951.

French, Roger, and Andrew Wear, eds. *The Medical Revolution of the Seventeenth Century*. Cambridge: Cambridge University Press, 1989.

Fuller, James F. "The Trial of Florence Newton." *Cork Historical and Archeological Society* 10 (1904).

Gentlemen's Magazine, 81 (1811) and (August 1911).

Glanvill, Joseph. *A Blow at Modern Sadducism*. London, 1668.

———. *Touching Florence Newton, Sadducismus Triumphatus*. London, 1681.

Godfrey, Sir Edmundbury. *Letters from Sir Edmundbury Godfrey, & Others*. MS. 4728, National Library of Ireland, Dublin.

Goodbody, Olive C. *Guide to Irish Quaker Records*. Dublin: Stationery Office for the Irish Manuscripts Commission, 1967.

Graham Manuscripts. Appendix to Historical Manuscripts Commission Report 6, 1877, National Library of Ireland, Dublin.

Granger, J. *Biographical History of England.* London, 1824.

Greatrakes, Valentine. *A Brief Account.* London, 1666.

——— . Letter to Robert Boyle from port of Minehead. 1668. Royal Society, BL, III. 21.

——— . Letter to the Bishop of Chester. Bodleian B 158, British Library, London. Lincoln.

Greenslet, Ferris. *Joseph Glanvill: A Study in English Thought and Letters of the Seventeenth Century.* New York: Columbia University Press, 1900.

Grosart, Alexander. *Lismore Papers.* First Series, vols. 2, 3, and 5, 1886; Second Series, vols. 1 and 2. 1887.

Harleian MSS. 3785, fol. 109. British Library, London.

Harris, Walter. *The History of the Writers of England.* Dublin, 1764.

Hatton Family. *Correspondence of the Hatton Family.* Edited by E. M. Thompson. Camden Society, 1878.

Hayman, Samuel (the Rev.). "Notes on the Family of Greatrakes." *Reliquary Quarterly Archeological Society* (London) 14 (1863).

——— . *The Illustrated Guide to the Blackwater and Ardmore.* Youghal, Ireland: W. G. Field, 1898.

Hist. MSS. Comm. Rep. Egmont MSS. Vol. 1. 1905.

Hist. MSS. Comm. Rep. Exeter City MSS. 1916. pp. 329, 334, 335, and 336.

Hunter, Richard A., and Ida Macalpine. *Valentine Greatraks and divers of the Strange Cures By him lately Performed on Patients from St. Bartholomew's Hospital in 1666: Three Hundred Years of Psychiatry.* London: Oxford University Press, 1963.

Jackson, C. J., ed. *The Diary of Abraham de la Pryme.* Surtees Society, 1870.

Jacob, J. R. *Henry Stubbe, Radical Protestantism and the Early Enlightenment.* Cambridge: Cambridge University Press, 1983.

——— . *Robert Boyle and the English Revolution.* New York: Burt Franklin, 1977.

Kaplan, Barbara. "Greatrakes the Stroker: The Interpretation of His Contemporaries." *Isis* 73 (1982).

Kearney, H. F. "Richard Boyle, Ironmaster." *Royal Society of Antiquaries of Ireland* 82 (1952).

Langston, C. J. "Lady Conway and Valentine Greatrakes, the Stroker." *Argosy* (London) 30 (1880).

Laver, A. Bryan. "Miracles No Wonders: The Mesmeric Phenomena and Organic Cures of Valentine Greatrakes." *Journal of the History of Medicine* 33 (1978).

Lewis, Samuel. *Topographical Dictionary of Ireland.* London, 1837.

Lloyd, David. *Wonders No Miracles.* London, 1666.

MacCarthy-Morrogh, Michael. *The Munster Plantation.* Oxford: Clarendon Press, 1986.

MacLysaght, E. *Calendar of Orrery Papers.* Dublin: Irish Manuscript Commission, 1941.

——— . *Irish Life in the Seventeenth Century: After Cromwell.* Dublin: Talbot Press, 1939.

Madden, R. R. *Some Notices of the Irish Mesmerists of the Seventeenth Century.* 1847.

Madden, T. M. "Revival of Some Old Fallacies Bearing on Medicine." *Dublin Journal of Medical Science* (July 1890).

Maddison, R. E. W. *The Life of the Honourable Robert Boyle.* London: Taylor & Francis, 1969.

Masson, Flora. *Robert Boyle.* London: Constable and Company, 1914.

Maxwell, C. *Stranger in Ireland.* London: Johnathan Cape, 1954.

McCarthy, Justin H. *A Short History of Ireland.* New York: John B. Alden, 1890.

McKeon, Michael. *Politics and Poetry in Restoration England*. Boston: Harvard University Press, 1975.

MSS. of the House of Lords. News Series. Vol. 3. London, 1905.

Muggleton, Ludovic. *The Acts of the Witnesses*. London, 1699.

Muir Mackenzie, Therese (Therese Villiers-Stuart). *Dromana: The Memoirs of an Irish Family*. Dublin: Sealy, Bryers & Walker, no date.

Mulholland, John. *Notes on Settlements at Rossmire, Co. Waterford*. Old Waterford Decies: Old Waterford Society, 1979.

Murphy, Denis (the Rev.). *Cromwell in Ireland*. Dublin: M. H. Gill & Son, 1897.

Murphy, Sean. *The Comeraghs: Fact and Fancy*. Waterford: Dunarvan Observer, 1974.

Murray's Handbook for Travellers in Ireland. London: John Cooke, 1902.

Nicolson, Marjorie. *The Conway Letters*. New Haven, Conn.: Yale University Press, 1930.

Notes and Queries, June 27, 1857, 510; May 14, 1864, 399; May 28, 1864, 447; June 7, 1864, 458–459; June 11, 1864; January 26, 1884, 61–63; April, 1953, 173; July 1953, 315; October 1953, 453; September 1954, 408–409, 545.

O'Brien, Eoin, Anne Crookshank, and Gordon Wolstenholme. *A Portrait of Irish Medicine, Published for the Bicentenary of the Royal College of Surgeons in Ireland*. Dublin: Ward River Press, 1984.

Oldenburg, Henry. *The Correspondence of Henry Oldenburg*. Vol. 2. Edited by A. Rupert Hall and Marie Boas Hall. Madison: University of Wisconsin Press, 1966.

Penn, William. *My Irish Journal*. Edited by Isabel Grubb. London: Longmans, Green & Co., 1952.

Person of Quality. *Rebels No Saints*. London, 1661.

Power, Patrick (the Very Reverend Canon). "The Ancient Highway of the Decies." *Royal Society of Antiquaries of Ireland* (1903).

————. *The Place Names of Decies.* London: David Nutt, 1907.

————. *Waterford & Lismore: A Compendious History of the United Dioceses.* Dublin: Cork University Press, 1937.

Power, Patrick C. "A Faith Healer of the 1600s." *Ireland's Eye,* September 1990.

————. *History of Waterford City and County.* Cork: Mercier Press, 1991.

Powys, Llewelyn. *Life and Times of Anthony à Wood.* London: Oxford University Press, 1961.

Prendergast, John P. *The Cromwellian Settlement.* Dublin: Mellifont Press, 1922.

Redmond, Gabriel O'Connell. "The Castles in North-East Cork, and Near Its Borders." *Journal of the Cork Historical and Archeological Society* 24 (1918).

Robbins, Keith, ed. *Religion and Humanism: The Ecclesiastical History Society.* London: Basil Blackwell, 1981.

Royal Comm. on Hist. MSS. Eighth Rep. App. 1881. British Library, London.

"Rub for Rub." London, 1666. Lutt. II, 183. British Library, London.

Ryan, Richard. *Worthies of Ireland.* Dublin: M. N. Mahon and R. Milliken, 1819.

Ryland, R. H. (the Rev.). *History, Topography and Antiquities of the City and County of Waterford.* Kilkenny, Ireland: Welbrook Press, 1982.

Saint-Evremond, Charles de. *The Irish Prophet: The Works of Monsieur Evremond.* London, 1723.

Seymour, St. John D. *The Puritans in Ireland.* Oxford: Oxford Historical and Literary Studies, 1921.

————. *Irish Witchcraft and Demonology.* Dublin: Hodges Figgis, 1913.

Sheehan, Anthony J. "The Population of the Plantation in Munster." *Cork Historical Society Journal* 87 (1982).

Shepherd, Francis J. "Medical, Quacks, and Quackeries." *Popular Science*, June 1883.

Smalbroke, Richard D. *A Vindication of the Miracles of Our Blessed Saviour*. London, 1724.

Smith, Charles. *The Antient and Present State of the County and City of Waterford*. Dublin, 1774.

Southey, Robert, and S. T. Coleridge. *Omniana*. London: Centaur Press, 1969.

Stapelton, T. A. "The Stroker." *Ireland's Own* magazine, August 31, 1946.

Steneck, Nicholas. "Greatrakes the Stroker: The Interpretation of Historians." *Isis* 73, no. 2 (1982).

Stubbe, Henry. *The Miraculous Conformist*. London, 1666.

Stowe Coll., 747, F. 112. British Library, London.

Townshend, Dorothea. *Life and Letters of the Great Earl of Cork*. London: Duckworth, 1904.

Walsh, Peter. *The History of the Irish Remonstrance*. London, 1674.

Ward, John (the Rev.). *Diary of Rev. John Ward*. Arranged by Charles Severn. London, 1839.

Wilson, D. " Valentine Greatrakes: Ophthalmologist." *Transactions of the Ophthalmological Society (U.K.)* (1967).

"Wonders if not Miracles, or, a relation of the wonderful performances of Valentine Gertrux of Affane near Youghall in Ireland, who cureth all manners of diseases with a stroke of his hand and prayer as is testified by many ear and eye witnesses." London, 1665.

Wood, Anthony à. *Athenae Oxonienses*. London, 1691.